COPYRIGHT

Rhythms of Grace: a Journey int
Study. Copyright © 2022 Kate Waterman. Cover design ©
Kate Waterman.

All rights reserved. No part of this book may be reproduced in any form or by any means without permission from the author.

All Scripture quotations, unless otherwise indicated, are taken from the Holy Bible, New International Version® Anglicized, NIV® Copyright © 1979, 1984, 2011 by Biblica, Inc.® Used by permission. All rights reserved worldwide. Capitalising of pronouns relating to the Father, Son and Holy Spirit are by the author, and may differ from the publisher's style.

Scripture quotations marked (MSG) are taken from The Message, copyright © 1993, 2002, 2018 by Eugene H. Peterson. Used by permission of NavPress. All rights reserved. Represented by Tyndale House Publishers, Inc.

Scripture quotations marked (NLT) are taken from the Holy Bible, New Living Translation, copyright ©1996, 2004, 2015 by Tyndale House Foundation. Used by permission of Tyndale House Publishers, Carol Stream, Illinois 60188. All rights reserved.

Scripture quotations marked (NKJV) are taken from the New King James Version®. Copyright © 1982 by Thomas Nelson. Used by permission. All rights reserved.

RESOURCES

Resources on the website are correct at time of writing (Spring 2022) but may be subject to change.

DISCLAIMER

All references to nations or geographical locations are to the historical people-groups and territories mentioned in the Bible, and do not in any way refer to countries, nations or places in the present day.

COVER PHOTO CREDITS

Bruce Mars (man at window); Alora Griffiths (woman in field); Eberhard Grossgasteiger (sky) @ unsplash.com, permitted use.

To my wonderful family, with all my love.

'Are you tired? Worn out? Burned out on religion?

Come to me. Get away with me and you'll recover your life.

I'll show you how to take a real rest.

Walk with me and work with me-watch how I do it.

Learn the unforced rhythms of grace'.

[Matthew 11:28 MSG]

WELCOME

Welcome!

I am so pleased to welcome you to the pages of this book.

My name is Kate Waterman, and I live in the UK in a beautiful area of northern England. I am a wife, mother and grandmother, an ex-primary school teacher and a social carer—roles which have given me quite a fund of stories and life-lessons. But the most important thing to know about me is that it is my faith-journey which has given me the keys to living in rest—keys that I want to share with you.

So many people live lives that are full of stress; difficult circumstances, overloaded diaries, unresolved issues, and doubts about self-worth are just some of the things which weigh them down. Perhaps you are one of them? And perhaps you dream of a deep peace, a profound rest taking root inside, which will allow you to live differently? The good news is that there is a way…

My own pursuit of this dream began as a young student teacher. Insecure and filled with self-doubt, I was happy enough with my skills, but not quite so sure about how I rated as a person. I was also frequently worried and fearful, plagued with feelings of guilt, and a chronic perfectionist. Although I became expert at 'stuffing' it all down—so other people wouldn't notice—unfortunately such junk tends to leak out at inappropriate moments!

And so, the quest began to 'live free'. Shortly after starting teacher-training, I had a profound encounter with God, and with it my perspective, and my experience, started to change, bit by bit. Transformation is always a process, rather than an overnight deal; revelation can happen in an instant, but walking it out, learning new habits and changing mindsets takes time.

Over the years I have learned how to live in increasing degrees of rest—in who I am, and in my circumstances—and out of that rest to live a fruitful life—and I'm still growing. The website, Rhythms of Grace: a Journey into Rest, which is found at https://www.rhythmsofgraceuk.org, is the story of that process—lessons I have learned from my personal journey, and from the countless stories shared with me, in many years of counselling and pastoral care. As the website contains a vast amount of reading material, this book is a response to those who wanted to access it in book form, and as a study course. The first two sections of the website are covered here, with additional material.

I want to invite you to join me on this walk to freedom, so I can share with you the keys I have learned, in order that you too can come into a place of deep rest and peace—and live the life you were created for.

Kate Waterman

CONTENTS

WELCOME 9

INTRODUCTION 13

SECTION 1

1. FOUNDATIONS FOR BIBLICAL REST 21
2. BUILDING A PERSONAL RELATIONSHIP WITH GOD 23
3. A BRAND-NEW LIFE 29
4. FIVE STEPS TO RESTORE MY RELATIONSHIP WITH GOD 35
5. WASHING THE PAST AWAY: THE GRACE OF BAPTISM 39
6. THE POWER OF BIBLICAL BAPTISM 49
7. THE HOLY SPIRIT AND YOU 57
8. FUEL FOR THE JOURNEY 1 65
9. THE POWER OF THE CROSS 69
10. MISSING THE MARK: OVERCOMING GUILT AND SHAME 77
11. FUEL FOR THE JOURNEY 2 87

12. GOD'S PROMISE OF PROVISION 91

13. EXPERIENCING GOD'S PRESENCE 99

14. PSALM 91 109

15. FURTHER NOTES ON FEAR 119

16. WHO AM I REALLY? 127

17. WHERE DO WE COME FROM? 137

18. FUEL FOR THE JOURNEY 3 147

SECTION 2

19. CREATING NEW MINDSETS 153

20. THE POWER OF THE SPOKEN WORD 165

21. CHOOSING GRATITUDE 176

22. NOTES ON DISCERNMENT 184

CONCLUSION

INTRODUCTION

Are you feeling…

- at the bottom of the heap?
- tired and worn out?
- easily overwhelmed?
- your life has no meaning?
- separated from God?
- oppressed or discouraged?

Maybe you are wrestling with…

- feelings of guilt, shame and anxiety?
- long-standing problems?
- identity or self-worth issues?
- constant worry and fear?
- unmet needs

Or maybe you are just tired of struggling and striving…

You're in the right place. This book (and the website it is derived from) was made just for you—out of the conviction that there is an answer, a way to be at peace; a way to find a

INTRODUCTION

place of rest. You can live free. Welcome to a journey of faith…

Jesus of Nazareth said:

> *"Thank You, Father, Lord of heaven and earth. You've concealed your ways from sophisticates and know-it-alls, but spelled them out clearly to ordinary people. Yes, Father, that's the way You like to work. Are you tired? Worn out? Burned out on religion? Come to Me. Get away with Me and you'll recover your life. I'll show you how to take a real rest. Walk with Me and work with Me—watch how I do it. Learn the unforced rhythms of grace. I won't lay anything heavy or ill-fitting on you. Keep company with Me and you'll learn to live freely and lightly." [Matthew 11:26-30, MSG]*

Jesus was a man totally at rest.

- He knew who He was; He was absolutely secure in His identity
- He was convinced of His purpose and destiny
- He had an intimate relationship with God the Father
- He walked in absolute alignment with the Father
- He was never fearful or worried; even when His life was in danger

- He was never overwhelmed, even when everyone wanted a piece of Him
- He would not allow the Evil One to oppress Him
- He had a totally clear conscience

- He had absolute confidence that whatever He needed, the Father would provide
- He knew He had God-given authority for every situation
- He always lived in the power and flow of the Spirit

Wouldn't you like to live the same way?

When Jesus died on the cross, He opened up the way for you to enter His rest; to learn to live the way He did; and to slip behind the 'veil' into the presence of God. This book will help you on that journey…

WHY 'RHYTHMS OF GRACE'?

A few years ago, I felt a strong compulsion to start recording the many lessons learned on my faith-journey. After praying, (which simply means talking to God in a conversational way, and listening for His answers), I woke up one morning with a phrase running through my head, and the clear conviction I was to set up a website with the name *'Rhythms of Grace: a Journey into Rest'*; and ideas started to flow regarding its content. Then a few days later, I came across *The Message Translation* of Matthew 11:28 (see above), which I had never read before, and found that the verse fits the theme perfectly. Eugene Peterson, the writer of *The Message* captures something beautifully in his interpretation. Rhythms of Grace website continued to evolve, (the present edition having been revised and extensively enlarged) and gave rise to this version in paperback format, with added resources for individual or group study. I hope you enjoy it!

INTRODUCTION

WHAT ARE 'THE UNFORCED RHYTHMS OF GRACE'?

When the Bible talks about God's grace, it is referring to His unmerited favour; favour that flows from His heart of love towards us. We can't earn it; we'll never deserve it—it's a wonderful free gift. Eugene Peterson expresses something profound when he talks about the 'rhythms' of that free-flowing grace.

There are four particular aspects of grace-filled rhythm which speak of the values which underpin the journey into God's rest.

'Rhythm' is derived from the Greek word for 'flow'. We often talk about rhythm in connection with a dance. While there is opportunity for spontaneity and self-expression, it is the music which gives the channel to flow in. We are invited into the great dance of Heaven, to let the music of Heaven fill us, with the Holy Spirit as our lead-partner. Rest is getting in the flow of the Spirit; being Spirit-led, and joyous.

Rhythm is a repeated sound. Throughout the Bible there is the sound of the Voice of God calling us into relationship; words of love and belonging; a Voice telling us who we are, and what we can be. This journey is not just about right practices or beliefs; it is about responding to a real voice; having an encounter with a real person. We are passionately loved, and despite all our failures and shortcomings, a way has been made for us to live in intimate relationship with our Heavenly Father. Rest comes through hearing and responding to the repeated sound of our Father's voice.

Rhythm is a repeated pattern. And one of the primary repeated patterns in Scripture is the provision of God. Over and over, we see the promise of His supply—material, physical, spiritual and emotional—and the outworking of it in the lives of ordinary people. The measure of rest we have in our lives is equal to our understanding of that provision—which had its ultimate fulfilment in Jesus—and we are invited to take hold of everything His life, death, resurrection and ascension has purchased for us. Imagine: all our needs, past, present and future being met…

Or to change the metaphor, drummers talk about getting into a 'groove' when the beat takes over, and they get into the flow. This is the answer to struggling and striving—we need to clear 'boulders' out of the way and get into the flow of the Spirit. Rest is based on seeing and receiving the repeated patterns of God's love and provision in our lives.

Rhythm often includes an off-beat, a responding note. Grace is not just about receiving. A pool which just receives water will become stagnant in time; there has to be an outflow to keep the water healthy. The 'off-beat' is our response to grace; moment by moment, taking what has been given and letting it flow out to others. 'Freely you have received, freely give,' commanded Jesus. We are to live lives which leak grace everywhere we go. Rest is grace-filled action, given freely, our response to love.

INTRODUCTION

JOURNEY MAP

Rhythms Of Grace, the website, is divided into sections. Section 1, *Foundations for Biblical Rest*, and Section 2, *Creating New Mindsets* are included in this book. Section 3, *The Privilege of Kingdom Living*, will be published in this format at a later date.

Each chapter follows the content of the website, with a few minor changes, ending with scope for a personal response based on the grace-filled rhythms outlined above:

>**HEAR AND RESPOND** to the voice of God
>
>**RECEIVE** His wonderful provision
>
>**GET IN THE FLOW** of His Spirit
>
>**GIVE FREELY** because you are blessed

GOING DEEPER

In order to get the most out of *Rhythms of Grace: a Journey into Rest* it is important to give time to meditate on, and digest each chapter. In view of this, most chapters also have a *Going Deeper* section for further reflection.

The book also includes three *Fuel for the Journey* sections which suggest good habits to develop on the way to your goal, and two *Notes On* chapters, which contain material published in pdf form on the website. In addition, a variety of supplementary resources are mentioned which can be accessed through https://www.rhythmsofgraceuk.org.

Rhythms of Grace: the Book is designed to be used as a

'discipleship track' for individuals, pairs or groups, in whichever way seems appropriate. If used in a group, perhaps personal reflection could be done prior to gatherings, and two or three key questions discussed together.

SECTION 1

CHAPTER 1

FOUNDATIONS FOR BIBLICAL REST

INTRODUCTION

In common understanding, rest is the freedom from exertion, action or movement, and involves leisure, relaxation, and sleep. We have whole industries devoted to promoting the benefits of these elements, yet the rest that comes from internal peace often remains elusive, and it is this rest that we need if we are to deal with the stress and worry of modern living.

A PERMANENT SOLUTION

If we want a permanent solution to our stress-filled lives, rather than a sticking plaster, we need to dig deep...

The media is full of advice for those who are tired of struggling, and while many of these suggestions are useful, they often don't deal with the underlying causes. If we truly want to achieve internal calm and spiritual peace, we need to put in the proper groundwork..

FOUNDATIONS FOR BIBLICAL REST

Just as it's vital that the foundations of a house are fashioned to take its weight, so we must pay attention to the important truths which underpin a life of rest.

Each chapter in this section discusses one of these foundational truths. Do take time to reflect on the content, even if it is familiar territory, as there are always fresh revelations waiting for us.

As you begin this journey out of a stress-filled life, be encouraged that you are not making it alone. Not only are you in the company of many others, you also have the promise of God Himself:

'My presence will go with you, and I will give you rest'
[Exodus 33:14].

SOMETHING TO PONDER

What is the cause of the most stress and unrest in your life at the moment?

- feelings of being overwhelmed?
- continual worries and fears?
- long-standing personal issues?
- the inability to get over past trauma?
- low self-esteem?
- relationship troubles?
- church-related issues?
- work anxieties?
- something else?

CHAPTER 2

BUILDING A PERSONAL RELATIONSHIP WITH GOD

True rest starts with re-establishing our place in the universe. We were designed not only to live in community with other people, but to have a personal relationship with God: to experience His presence, know His unfailing love, and enjoy His supernatural provision. To live outside that fundamental relationship leaves a void that cannot otherwise be filled.

The problem we face is that there seems to be an enormous gulf between humankind, and the almighty God, Lord of the universe. This sense of separation from God has to be dealt with…

WHY DO WE FEEL SEPARATED FROM GOD?

Our problem is a guilty conscience; every one of us has missed the mark:

- We have all said or done things we shouldn't have

- We all regret having failed to do other things
- We have all made poor choices at times
- We have all got little habits and idiosyncrasies, which we would rather keep hidden
- We have all had thoughts which we would not like to become public

All these things have a price tag. Not only do they affect our inner peace, and our relationships with other people; they separate us from a holy and majestic God.

Who can free us from our history of failure? How can we stop feeling guilty? How can we feel clean inside?

JESUS TOOK OUR PUNISHMENT

A holy and righteous God cannot ignore the way man's wrongdoing has ruined His creation; He cannot just say it doesn't matter and turn a blind eye. For Him to do right, that sin has to be judged and punished.

Amazingly, God found a way to satisfy His holiness and yet spare you and me the consequences of our failures.

The Bible reveals that there is one God, but He is known to man in three different forms: God the Father, God the Son, and God the Holy Spirit, (rather like H_2O can refer to water, steam or ice—a simple analogy of a profound truth). So, when I talk about Jesus or the Holy Spirit in this book, I am talking about *God Himself*.

As Jesus, God Himself came to earth in human flesh, fully human, and yet without sin. He chose to stand in our place and take the consequences of our failures on our behalf. As He hung upon the cross, Jesus took all of our wrongdoing, all of our mistakes and shortfall, on Himself. For hour after hour, He suffered the judgement, written into the laws of the universe since the beginning of time, upon every evil, big or small, which has ever been perpetrated. As He breathed His last breath, He cried out, 'It is finished!' [John 19:30]. There was nothing left, not one single thing, standing in the way of you and me having a relationship with God.

A SIMPLE ANALOGY

I am reminded of a simple story I heard many years ago when I was a teenager. The speaker, whose name I can't remember, described an incident with his children:

His young daughter had refused to eat the poached egg prepared for her breakfast. In response, her father decided that as it had been specially prepared for her, she was not to get up from the table until it was eaten.

The daughter was a strong-willed little girl, and sat... and sat... and sat. And so the result was a stand-off between father and child—and an unpleasant atmosphere in the house. Distressed at the relationship breakdown he was witnessing, the little girl's older brother decided to take action; he sat down and ate the cold egg himself!

As the issue that was standing between them had been dealt with, there was no longer any reason to prevent father and daughter being friends again. And peace returned.

A simple story, but a profound illustration...

Jesus took everything which causes our separation from

BUILDING A PERSONAL RELATIONSHIP WITH GOD

God upon Himself, taking the consequences for our sin in our place, in order that our fellowship with God could be restored.

You can read the story of Jesus' death in the Gospel of John, chapters 19 and 20.

The Greek word for 'forgive' in the New Testament means 'to send away'.

Just imagine…

- All those things I've thought, said or done, that I wished I hadn't
- All those things I should have done
- All those things I could have done, and didn't
- All those mistakes I've made
- All those poor choices
- All the times I've fallen short of my expectations, and those of other people
- All the guilt and shame I've ever experienced

All the mess I've made from my beginning to this moment—and then on into the future; everything has been dealt with by Jesus. Forgiveness is mine for the asking.

Why not take some time to be quiet, and consider the first step on your journey into rest right now?

RHYTHMS OF GRACE

HEAR AND RESPOND to the voice of God

Get very quiet inside and reflect. What makes you feel guilty? Relationships? Mistakes? Poor choices? Things you have done, or think you should have done?

Identifying and facing up to these feelings is a big deal—and the first step to healing.

RECEIVE His wonderful provision

Jesus' death bridged the gap between Heaven and earth; between you and God.

In order to benefit from His sacrifice, and take your unique place in the universe, you need to personally receive this wonderful provision.

You can find out how to do that in the next chapter.

GET IN THE FLOW of His Spirit

If you have already taken this step, take some time to reflect on the amazing gift you have been given… and let your praises flow.

GOING DEEPER: PERSONAL OR GROUP STUDY

1. What does biblical rest look like? How is it different from the kind of rest often promoted by the media or self-help industry?

2. Why do people feel separated from God? Have you experienced that feeling?

3. What was God's solution? If Jesus is God Himself, what does this solution tell you about the nature of God?

4. Why do you think some people have a hard time receiving forgiveness? What would you say to them on the basis of what you have read?

CHAPTER 3

A BRAND-NEW LIFE

I WANT TO DO WHAT IS RIGHT, BUT I CAN'T

The freedom which comes from being forgiven is wonderful, but it doesn't stop there... because what I really need, to be at rest in my body, soul and spirit, is a brand-new me!

Jesus' death didn't only deal with my shortfall, it dealt with me. I do wrong because there is something inside of me that is wrong. I think we can all identify with the words of the apostle Paul:

> *I want to do what is right, but I can't. I want to do what is good, but I don't. I don't want to do what is wrong, but I do it anyway [Romans 7:18-19 NLT].*

God knows that if left to my own devices I will continue to fail, so when Jesus died, He not only took my sins and failures upon Himself, He took the very essence of me (and you) as well. My human propensity to sin was put to death with Him [Romans 6:6]. This doesn't mean I will never sin again, but that the core issue was dealt with on the Cross.

A BRAND-NEW LIFE

RESURRECTION LIFE

But even that isn't the end of the story, because Jesus didn't stay dead...

In the book, *The Lion, the Witch and the Wardrobe*,[1] Aslan the good Lion King, sacrificed his life for a young boy who had betrayed his friends and family to their enemy, the wicked White Witch. We join the story where his two young friends are mourning his death...

(Susan and Lucy) walked to the eastern edge of the hill and looked down. The one big star had almost disappeared. The country looked dark grey, but beyond, at the very end of the world, the sea showed pale. The sky began to turn red... At that moment they heard from behind them a loud noise—a great cracking, deafening noise... The rising of the sun had made everything look so different – all colours and shadows were changed – that for a moment they didn't see the important thing. Then they did. The Stone Table was broken into two pieces by a great crack that ran down it from end to end; and there was no Aslan...

"Oh, oh, oh!" cried the two girls, rushing back to the Table.

"Oh it's too bad," sobbed Lucy; "they might have left his body alone."

"Who's done it?" cried Susan. "What does it mean? Is it magic?"

"Yes!" said a great voice behind their backs. "It is more magic." They looked round. There, shining in the sunrise, larger than they had seen him before, shaking his mane (for it had apparently grown again) stood Aslan himself.

"Aren't you dead then, dear Aslan?" said Lucy.

"Not now," said Aslan.

"But what does it all mean?" asked Susan when they were somewhat calmer.

"It means," said Aslan, "that though the Witch knew the Deep Magic, there is a magic deeper still which she did not know. Her knowledge goes back only to the dawn of time. But if she could have looked a little farther back, into the stillness and the darkness before Time dawned, she would have read there a different incantation. She would have known that when a willing victim who had committed no treachery was killed in a traitor's stead, the Table would crack and Death itself would start working backward."…

"Oh, children," said the Lion, "I feel my strength coming back to me. Oh, children, catch me if you can!" He stood for a second, his eyes very bright, his limbs quivering, lashing himself with his tail. Then he made a leap high over their heads and landed on the other side of the Table. Laughing, though she didn't know why, Lucy scrambled over it to reach him… A mad chase began… It was such a romp as no one has ever had in Narnia… And the funny thing was then when all three finally lay together panting in the sun the girls no longer felt in the least tired or hungry or thirsty.

"And now," said Aslan presently, "to business. I feel I am going to roar. You had better put your fingers in your ears."

This is a beautiful allegory about Jesus, who was sacrificed in our place, to enable us to be reconciled to God. But like the lion in the story, He didn't stay dead. The Bible teaches that He rose again from the dead, and is still alive. (You can read about His resurrection in John 20.)

A BRAND-NEW LIFE

BEGIN AGAIN THROUGH BEING 'IN CHRIST'

We were included in that death and resurrection.

Watchman Nee,[2] a well-known Chinese Christian writer, used the illustration of a ticket placed in a book: whether you send the book across the country, put it in a dark cellar, or take to the top of the highest skyscraper, the ticket goes too. Wherever the book is, the ticket is as well.

This is what it means to be 'in Christ'.

So as the 'ticket in the book', when Jesus died, the old me died too. But in the same way, when Jesus rose from the dead...

By trusting in Jesus' death to deal with my sins, and His resurrection to give me new life, I can begin again. This is the real source of internal peace.

And that's how we get a brand-new start. Not only has God wiped the slate clean of our shortfall, He has made us brand-new people, new creations. This is what being 'born again' means.

> *I have been crucified with Christ and I no longer live, but Christ lives in me. The life I now live in the body, I live by faith in the Son of God, who loved me and gave Himself for me [Galatians 2:20].*

> *Therefore, if anyone is in Christ, the new creation has come: the old has gone, the new is here! [2 Corinthians 5:17].*

And, what's more…

When we were 'born again', we were born into a different kingdom—we are now citizens of the Kingdom of

God.

> *For He has rescued us from the dominion of darkness and brought us into the kingdom of the Son He loves [Colossians 1:13].*

Jesus has done everything necessary to make it possible for you and me to live a different sort of life. Our part is to stop battling with self-improvement, put our lives in His hands, and receive the free gift He is offering.

RHYTHMS OF GRACE

If you need a brand-new start today…

HEAR AND RESPOND to the voice of God

Take the steps described in the next chapter.
And if you took these steps long ago…

GET IN THE FLOW of His Spirit

Turn your heart towards the Lord who has saved you, be amazed again at His grace, and let your praises flow

GOING DEEPER: PERSONAL OR GROUP STUDY

1. If you haven't done so recently, read *'The Lion, the Witch and the Wardrobe'* or watch the film. What do you learn about 'Aslan'? Why do you think C. S. Lewis chose a lion to represent Jesus?

2. Read the accounts of the death and resurrection of Jesus in John 19 and 20, slowly and meditatively. (If you wish, you can use the method described in Fuel for the Journey 3.) What particularly strikes you from each story?

3. What did Jesus accomplish through His death and resurrection?

4. The phrase 'in Christ' is found several times in the epistles. What does it mean?

5. What takes place when people are 'born again'?

END NOTES

[1]CS Lewis, (2009) *The Lion, the Witch and the Wardrobe*, Harper Collins Children's Books 1st ed.

[2]Watchman Nee, (2009) *The Normal Christian Life*, CLC Publications

CHAPTER 4

FIVE STEPS TO RESTORE MY RELATIONSHIP WITH GOD

Take some time to re-read and absorb the last two chapters, before taking the steps outlined below.

And check out these passages from the Bible…

- 1 John 1:9
- 1 John 4:14-15
- John 3:16
- Ephesians 2:8-9
- 1 John 5:12-13

Then take these five steps:

Find a quiet spot, then focus your attention on the Lord, and ask Him to come close. Speak each of the following (or something similar) aloud. Verbalising your convictions is surprisingly important—you can read an explanation of this in the chapter on 'The Power of the Spoken Word'.

WASHING THE PAST AWAY: THE GRACE OF BAPTISM

ACKNOWLEDGE

I am a sinner. However hard I try, I always fall short of perfect, and so I am separated from God by my wrongdoing. I will never be good enough by my own efforts. I can't make it on my own; I need someone to come alongside me and help me.

BELIEVE

Jesus is the Son of God, who took every bit of my shortfall upon Himself, and took the punishment that I deserved. He has bridged the gap between me and God, so I can trust God to completely forgive me.

PRAY

> *Dear Jesus, I know that I have thought, and said, and done many wrong things, and there are many right things I have failed to do. (Speak out the ones which come to mind.) I know that even when I try really hard, I can't change myself. So, I accept the gift You are offering me—that You died in my place, taking my punishment so that I no longer need to struggle with separation from God. I choose to put my trust in You, and I ask You to take charge of my life. Amen.*

THANK

Thank You, Jesus, for dying for me. Thank You that I'm forgiven for everything I have ever done, every bit of shortfall, big and small. Thank You that I am free to know God personally. Thank You that I am a new creation, the old has gone and the new has come, and thank You for taking charge of my life. Help me to listen to Your voice and follow where You lead. Thank You Lord, this is the beginning of the rest of my life!

AND FINALLY…TELL SOMEONE!

Telling someone about the actions you have just taken, is a really important step in your transition to a new life. Why not write to me at journeyintorest@gmail.com, I would love to hear your news!

CHAPTER 5

WASHING THE PAST AWAY: THE GRACE OF BAPTISM

A crucial element in our journey into a new life of rest is water baptism. The deliberate action involved in full immersion is a profoundly important building block in our foundations.

To grasp why it is so vital, we need to understand a bit about its definition and history...

WATER BAPTISM: MEANING AND PURPOSE

The word 'baptism' comes from the Greek word 'baptizo', meaning immersion, and has the sense of something taking on the qualities of the solution it is immersed in, for example cloth in a dye.

Vines Expository Dictionary has this to say:

This word should not be confused with 'baptō'. The clearest example that shows the meaning of baptizo is a text from the Greek poet and physician Nicander, who lived about 200 B.C. It is a recipe for making pickles and is helpful because it uses both words. Nicander says that in order to make a pickle, the vegetable should first be *'dipped' (baptô)* into boiling water and then *'baptised' (baptizô)* in the vinegar solution. Both verbs concern the immersing of vegetables in a solution. But the first is temporary. The second, the act of baptising the vegetable, produces a permanent change.[1]

HISTORY OF BAPTISM

WATER FOR PURIFICATION

The idea of washing with water for purification is common to a number of religions, and was explicitly commanded in the Torah, the Jewish book of Law.

According to these precepts, any ceremonial or ritual uncleanness separated people from the wider community until they became 'clean' again, and prevented them from worshipping in the temple, or in the case of priests, prevented them from carrying out their priestly duties. Uncleanness could come from a variety of sources, including contact with a dead person or animal, serious skin diseases, sexual relations at proscribed times, childbirth, and contact with an unclean article or person. A state of uncleanness was therefore a regular experience in the normal course of everyday life.

By the time of Jesus, both public and private purification baths, called 'mikvahs' were commonly used for cleansing. Mikvahs used running (known as 'living') water, and full immersion was required for the candidate to be properly cleansed. Some devout Jews used them daily in anticipation of the coming Messiah.

WATER AS AN INITIATION RITE

In the ancient world, the use of water in initiation rites was also common, including for Jewish proselytes who, by the first century AD, were routinely baptised. The act signified the turning away from idolatry, as well as purification, consecration, and acceptance into the covenant community, giving the candidate the right to its privileges and blessings.

Some rabbis referred to the waters of baptism as 'the womb of the world' and the new convert as 'a little child just born', having been separated from his pagan past:

The proselyte who casts off the impurity of idolatry and turns to the God of life becomes a new creature... a proselyte is like a new-born child whose family relations are no longer the same as before his conversion.[2]

WATER BAPTISM FORESHADOWED

In addition to the practice of immersion for cleansing and initiation, the Old Testament also has illuminating stories which foreshadow the New Testament baptism of repentance, and rebirth.

Noah's Ark [Genesis 6-9]

Noah, (whose name means 'rest'!) and his family, passed through the waters of judgement, and became, in effect, new creations in a new world.

WASHING THE PAST AWAY: THE GRACE OF BAPTISM

Israel's Escape from Egypt [Exodus 14]

After the Israelites were rescued from Egypt by the Lord, they had to walk through the waters of the Red Sea, which divided to let them pass. In this way they crossed over from slavery to freedom, and became the redeemed covenant community of God.

Israel's Entry into the Promised Land [Joshua 3]

Joshua led the nation of Israel through the River Jordan to the Promised Land. The Ark of the Covenant, which hosted the Presence and Covenant of God, was held up on the shoulders of the priests in the water, while Israel passed safely through into their inheritance.

Naaman, the Leper [2 Kings 5]

The captain of Syria's army, Naaman, a Gentile, was healed of leprosy, which in the Bible, represents uncleanness, sin and separation from God. He was instructed by the prophet Elisha to wash seven times in the River Jordan. When he came up from the waters, his skin was like a 'little child's' (compare this to the rabbinic quotation above) and was perfectly clear.

BAPTISM IN THE NEW TESTAMENT

John the Baptist [Luke 3:1-22]

John the Baptist came to the River Jordan preaching a baptism of repentance, for the forgiveness of sins. The

Greek word for repentance here means a change of thinking, coupled with contrition and submission to the Lord.

'Change the way you think, align yourself with God's ways and thoughts', John challenged his hearers.

The Bible states that the reason John baptised with water was so that Jesus might be revealed to Israel [John 1:29-31]. The confession of sin and the alignment of the thought-life with God were the necessary requirements for that revelation. Moreover, the River Jordan was significant because it is the lowest river in elevation in the world; its name means 'descent'. Literally and symbolically, those coming to be baptised, were humbling themselves.

The religious people, however, were offended, thinking they had no need of repentance; after all, they belonged to God's chosen nation. These were the ones who were not able to 'see' Jesus, despite all His actions.

The Significance of Jesus' Baptism [Matthew 3:13-16]

Jesus also came to the river Jordan to be baptised, 'to fulfil all righteousness'. He came, not because He needed to repent, for He was fully aligned with the Father in every way, but to identify Himself with the condition of sinful man, and as a mark of His total commitment to the path He had chosen.

We have seen that priests had to use 'waters of purification' in order to be ceremonially clean for their duties. The book of Hebrews describes Jesus as a priest, in fact, the 'Great High Priest'; by 'washing' in the Jordan,

WASHING THE PAST AWAY: THE GRACE OF BAPTISM

Jesus was also symbolically preparing for that role.

And it was whilst being baptised that Jesus heard His Father's voice, saying, 'This is My beloved Son in whom I am well pleased'. As His heavenly Father gave Him public approval and affirmation, the foundation was laid for His extraordinary ministry.

When Jesus, in turn, commissioned His disciples, He gave the command:

> *'All authority in heaven and on earth has been given to Me. Therefore, go and make disciples of all nations, baptising them in the name of the Father and of the Son and of the Holy Spirit, and teaching them to obey everything I have commanded you. And surely I am with you always, to the very end of the age' [Matthew 28:18-20].*

RHYTHMS OF GRACE

HEAR AND RESPOND to the voice of God

Take some time to reflect on what you have read. In the next chapter you will discover more about why baptism is important in your quest to combat stress and find real rest.

GOING DEEPER: PERSONAL OR GROUP STUDY

Although there are a good number of points for reflection here, it is worth taking the time to work through them as baptism is such a significant step in the Christian journey. The more we understand, the more we will benefit.

Historical Context

1. Where do we get the word 'baptism' from? What does it mean? Why is it significant?

2. What do you think ceremonial uncleanness is? What kind of things made people ceremonially impure in the Judaism of Jesus' day? Why do you think water was chosen to deal with this 'problem'?

3. Baptism has been used in initiation rites for various religions, why do you think this is? What did baptism signify when used for Jewish proselytes?

Old Testament Stories

4. Read the four Old Testament stories. How was water the means of transition from one state or circumstance to another, for the characters in each story?

WASHING THE PAST AWAY: THE GRACE OF BAPTISM

Baptism in the Gospels

5. What is the underlying meaning of the Greek word for repentance? Why do you think it is important to align yourself with God's way of thinking? What might be the consequences of 'unaligned' thinking? List some practical examples.

6. Are there areas of your thought-life where you need to 'repent' and bring your thinking into line with the Lord? (For example, negative, fearful, critical or depressed thought-patterns are some which need re-alignment.)

7. Read Luke 3:1-22. What did John mean in verse 8 when he challenged his listeners:

'Produce fruit in keeping with repentance.'?

How do you think a change in thinking affects people's behaviour? Is it possible to change one without the other?

8. Why do you think the revelation of who Jesus is, is related to repentance?

9. What command did Jesus give to His disciples regarding baptism? Based on what you've read, why do you think He thought it was important?

END NOTES

[1] WE Vine, (1975) *Vines Expository Dictionary*, Oliphants, London

[2] http://www.jewishencyclopedia.com/articles/3321-birth-new

CHAPTER 6

THE POWER OF BIBLICAL BAPTISM

Nicodemus, a leading Pharisee, came to talk to Jesus one night [John 3:1-21]. Given what we have noted about converts to Judaism being described as 'new creations', and 'new-born children', he must have been startled to hear Jesus say that he too must be born again. After all, he was one of God's 'special people', and an important one at that. But Jesus was insistent, without new birth he could not see or enter the Kingdom of Heaven.

> *Jesus answered, 'Very truly I tell you, no one can enter the kingdom of God unless they are born of water and the Spirit' [John 3:5].*

And it seemed that baptism was a non-negotiable part of being born again. Nicodemus, like any other convert, would have to humble himself and be baptised.

BAPTISM IN THE NAME OF JESUS

As we have seen, John's baptism was a baptism of

repentance and forgiveness, Christian baptism includes those elements, but baptism 'in the Name of Jesus' is a baptism of faith in His work (Acts 19:3-5), that is, faith in His death and resurrection.

In Chapter 3, *A Brand New Life*, we saw that not only do we need forgiveness and cleansing from our shortfall, we also need to be set free from our natural propensity to sin (our sinful nature) and become brand-new people. Bearing in mind that the word 'baptism' (from the Greek 'baptizo') means immersion, when we go down into the water, we are enacting death and burial. That act declares our faith in Jesus' death on the cross on our behalf, and it also proclaims that by faith in Him, we have died to our old life. The old self has gone!

But of course, we don't stay down there; as we rise out of the water, we are enacting resurrection. Symbolically, we are declaring our faith in Jesus' resurrection, and our conviction that through Him, we have new life. The new self is here! (And with it, new instincts to live in a way which pleases God.)

> *We are those who have died to sin; how can we live in it any longer? Or don't you know that all of us who were baptised into Christ Jesus were baptised into His death? We were therefore buried with Him through baptism into death in order that, just as Christ was raised from the dead through the glory of the Father, we too may live a new life. [Romans 6:3-4]*

Of course, the more we understand what Jesus has accomplished on the cross, the more we will appreciate the power and significance of water baptism. Although we can spend the rest of our lives studying this life-changing event and not begin to exhaust its wonders, some of the implications of the Cross will be explored in a later chapter.

BAPTISM AS A PROPHETIC ACT

A prophetic act is a physical action in time and space which declares a spiritual truth—not only to human onlookers, but also to spiritual powers (both angelic and demonic) in the heavenly realms. Prophetic acts have the power to release heavenly truth on earth.

As well as symbolising spiritual truth, baptism by immersion is also a prophetic act, demonstrating to the powers of darkness the wisdom of God, and causing a spiritual shift. We are instructed to release on earth that which has already been released in Heaven [Matthew 18:18]. Baptism does exactly that—it releases in our lives what has been purchased on our behalf in Heaven.

BAPTISM AS A TESTIMONY

Baptism is also a powerful declaration of faith to those watching. When we testify in word or action, to our belief in the name of Jesus, we stir faith in others to receive the same gift.

BENEFITS OF BIBLICAL BAPTISM

According to the Bible, when we are baptised in faith…

- We are 'born' of water', and are able to see and enter the Kingdom of Heaven [John 3:5]

- We are forgiven and our sins are washed away [Acts 22:14-16]

- We have a promise of a clear conscience before God [1 Peter 3:18-21]

- We have died, been buried, and are raised from the dead, with Christ [Colossians 2:9-12; Romans 6:2-7]

- We are spiritually 'circumcised'—our sinful nature is cut away [Colossians 2:9-12]

- We are given a new life [Titus 3:5]

- We are clothed with Christ [Galatians 3:26-27]

It also, by implication:

- Rescues us from the Kingdom of Darkness, and gives us a new Sovereign [Colossians 1:13]

- Consecrates us as part of a new priesthood [Leviticus 8:1-6; 1 Peter 2:9]

- Takes away our separation from God, and others [Ephesians 4:4-6]

- Marks our entry into the Covenant-community of God [Acts 2:41]

Water baptism is an essential foundation for our new stress-busting life. Do take time to re-read these chapters and reflect on the biblical references—even if you have already been baptised.[1]

Incidentally, nowhere in the New Testament does it say that that baptism has to be part of an official service, or presided over by a 'minister', for every believer is a priest [1 Peter 2:5,9]. All it needs is water, deep enough for immersion, and some other believers to baptise 'in the name of the Father, the Son and the Holy Spirit', and stand as witnesses, (2 or 3 witnesses being a good biblical standard).

However, it is a good reason for a party…

RHYTHMS OF GRACE

HEAR AND RESPOND to the voice of God

The Introduction describes how Jesus lived a life of perfect rest. He has opened up the way for you to live in the same manner…

- o Get really quiet inside.
- o Turn your heart towards the Lord.
- o Listen and respond to what He says.

GET IN THE FLOW of His Spirit

If you have already been baptised, take some time now to thank God for all its benefits.

GIVE FREELY because you are blessed

Ask the Lord to give you the opportunity to share the blessing of baptism with someone who needs it.

The next step on the journey into rest; is the empowerment to live your brand-new life, which will be discussed in the next chapter.

GOING DEEPER: PERSONAL OR GROUP STUDY

1. Read John 3:1-21. The Kingdom of God (or Heaven) refers to the rule and reign of God. What are the qualifications for 'seeing' or participating in the Kingdom, according to Jesus? What are the implications of His statement?

2. What was the purpose of John's baptism? How was baptism 'in the Name of Jesus' different?

3. Describe what takes place when we are baptised 'in the Name of Jesus'.

4. Read Romans 6:1-14. Do you need to add anything to your answer to question 3? In view of the truth expressed here, why do you think people continue to sin after being baptised? (You may need to revisit this question later on in your journey.)

5. Explain the difference between baptism as a prophetic act, and baptism as a testimony.

6. Read the relevant Scriptures, then personalise the 10 benefits of baptism:

*Through baptism I*_____.

7. What practical considerations do we need to consider, in order to be baptised, or to baptise someone else?

8. Is the Lord saying anything to you personally about this subject?

END-NOTES

[1]Please see the relevant page on the website for additional resources

CHAPTER 7

THE HOLY SPIRIT AND YOU

Please note *The Person and Work of the Holy Spirit* which appears as a separate webpage on the '*Rhythms of Grace*' website, is included in this chapter.

Through Jesus' death and resurrection, we have been given the opportunity for a brand-new start. However, as wonderful as a fresh start is, God knew that a clean sheet wasn't enough. The fact is, we can't measure up through our own efforts, however hard we try—we need right-living to flow naturally from the inside.

God said that He would do something new...

THE SPIRIT-FILLED LIFE

> *I will put My law in their minds and write it on their hearts. I will be their God, and they will be My people [Jeremiah 31:33].*

> *I will sprinkle clean water on you, and you will be clean; I will cleanse you from all your impurities and from all your idols. I will give you a new heart and put a new spirit in*

THE HOLY SPIRIT AND YOU

> *you; I will remove from you your heart of stone and give you a heart of flesh. And I will put My Spirit in you and move you to follow My decrees and be careful to keep My laws [Ezekiel 36:25-27].*

During His time on earth, Jesus had been alongside His disciples, showing the right way to live. But something even better was promised: the Law-giver would come to live *in* them—so that He could enable them to do right.

Jesus said,

> *'I will not leave you as orphans; I will come to you. Before long, the world will not see Me anymore, but you will see Me. Because I live, you also will live' [John 14:19].*

When Jesus ascended into Heaven, the Holy Spirit was released to earth in His place. And He didn't come just to anoint special people like those mentioned in the Old Testament, but to fill all who believe.

In the last days, God says,

> *'I will pour out My Spirit on all people. Your sons and daughters will prophesy, your young men will see visions, your old men will dream dreams. Even on My servants, both men and women, I will pour out My Spirit in those days, and they will prophesy' [Acts 2:17,18].*

The Holy Spirit is God Himself, not an impersonal power or a force, and He desires to fill us to overflowing, to enable us to live a new life—a Spirit-filled life—and for that life to spill over to touch our spheres of influence. Jesus opened the door for God's presence and power to be made available to all.

Sadly, many people have not heard that it is possible to ask for the Holy Spirit to come to them in this way; and they struggle to live a new life by their own willpower. To enter rest, we must avail ourselves of the whole package.

HOW CAN I BE FILLED WITH THE SPIRIT?

1. Be thirsty. Come just as you are, acknowledging your need of Him, and choosing to yield to His leadership [John 7: 37-38; Galatians 5:16].

2. Come to Jesus; He is the baptiser. Get very quiet inside, then turn the 'eyes of your heart' towards Him.

3. Ask Him to baptise (immerse) you in the Holy Spirit [John 1:32-34].

4. Believe you have received, because 'He who has promised is faithful' [Luke 11:9-13].

5. Thank God for His provision; for 'out of the overflow of the heart, the mouth speaks' [Luke 6:45, Berean Study Bible]. Start to praise, and the overflow will start to pour forth.

WHAT IF I ASK, AND IT SEEMS AS THOUGH NOTHING HAS HAPPENED?

As a teenager, I asked many times to be filled with the Spirit and got very discouraged because nothing appeared to have happened; that is, I had no physical manifestations. Eventually, a book I was reading transformed the situation.

Faith is based on God's Word, not on our circumstances or feelings. God said He would give the Holy Spirit to those who ask, [Luke 11:13]; I had asked—so He had given.

I began to thank Him for answering my prayer, despite having no 'evidence'. After about three days, I was overwhelmed with all the feeling I could possibly want. Why not try it and see!

RHYTHMS OF GRACE

RECEIVE His wonderful provision

Why not take the steps above right now? If you have already been baptised in the Spirit, you can always ask for more, as we need to be continually filled with the Spirit [Acts 4:31].

GIVE FREELY because you are blessed

Jesus said:

> *Whoever believes in Me, as Scripture has said, from his*

innermost being will flow rivers of living water' [John 7:38].

Now you have received this precious gift, find someone else who needs it, and lead them through the steps above. At step 2, put your hands on them, (if appropriate, and with their permission), and ask God to fill them with the Spirit, as He has filled you. Let that river flow!

MORE ON THE HOLY SPIRIT...

THE HOLY SPIRIT IS A PERSON

Scripture makes it clear that the Holy Spirit is not an impersonal force, energy or influence, but a Person.

Jesus used the personal masculine pronoun when speaking of Him [for example, John 14:15-16,26; 15:26-27; 16:7-14] and said the Spirit would come alongside the disciples as the Comforter—taking the place of Jesus.

Personal characteristics were attributed to Him—a will, thoughts, feelings and activity [for example, Matthew 4:1; 12:31-32; John 14:26; 16:8-11; Acts 13:2; Romans 8:26-27; 1 Corinthians 2:10-13; 12:11; Ephesians 4:30; Colossians 1:8; Isaiah 63:10].

Not only is the Holy Spirit a Person, but the Bible reveals Him to be the third member of the Trinity, the Godhead. Jesus clearly taught that the Spirit was one with the Father and Son [for example, John 14:16,26; 16:7-13], but was separate from them [John 1:33; 14:16,26; 15:26; Ephesians 2:18]. And Christians are commanded to baptise in the name of the Father, Son and the Holy Spirit [Matthew 8:19].

The Holy Spirit shows both divine attributes and actions, [for example, Luke 1:35; Romans 1:4; 8:11,26; Hebrews 9:14; 2 Peter 1:21; Genesis 1:1-2; Psalm 139:7-10] and is not to be treated casually. He is just as much Lord, as the Father and Son.

GETTING TO KNOW THE HOLY SPIRIT

If the Spirit of God is a person, rather than a force or power, we can get to know Him. These are some of the ways He works in our lives…

When the Holy Spirit comes to us, He brings:

- An outflow of life [John 7:38].
- Comfort and counsel [John 14:15-17].
- Instruction [John 14:25-26].
- Guidance, truth and revelation [John 16:13-15].
- Boldness [Acts 4:31].
- Power, which includes 'excellence of soul' in the meaning of the Greek word [Acts 1:8].
- Ability to pray [Romans 8:26].
- The character of Jesus [Galatians 5:22-23].

This is not an exhaustive list, there are many more blessings!

GOING DEEPER: PERSONAL OR GROUP STUDY

1. How would you describe the Holy Spirit?

2. Read the references in the section on the 'Work of the Holy Spirit'; then personalise His work in you:

Eg: The Holy Spirit makes rivers of living water flow from me...

3. Why do you think the Holy Spirit is essential to a life of rest?

4. Take the steps to be filled (or re-filled) with the Spirit. If studying this as part of a group, pray for each other; alternatively, ask God to show you someone else who needs to be filled with the Spirit, and lead them through the same steps, with their permission.

5. Get to know more about the Spirit through *Reflections on the Holy Spirit*, accessed from *The Person and Work of the Holy Spirit* page on the website. Take some time each day to meditate on the truth about His presence in your life.

CHAPTER 8

FUEL FOR THE JOURNEY 1

For those starting out…

To grow in your new relationship with God, you will need to develop some habits which will enable you to become strong in your faith.

Try out the suggestions below. It will take time and patience to establish them in your daily routine, but they will provide important foundations for the rest of your Christian life. More 'fuel' will feature later on in the study.

KEEP SHORT ACCOUNTS

> *If we confess our sins, He is faithful and just and will forgive us our sins and purify us from all unrighteousness [1 John 1:9].*

Your sin was taken care of, once and for all, through Jesus' death on the cross. However, it will take time to learn how to walk in your new life, and things will crop up each day which will reveal sinful attitudes, and make you feel guilty or ashamed. It is a good habit to end the day by asking the

FUEL FOR THE JOURNEY 1

Lord to remind you of things you have said, thought or done which have grieved Him.

- o Find a quiet spot and become really quiet inside.
- o Ask the Lord to come close to you. Thank Him for His presence.
- o Ask Him to show you anything that has grieved Him today.
- o Confess your sins and failings, without making excuses.
- o Ask Him to forgive you.
- o Thank Him that He has done just that.

Remember, faith is taking God at His word, regardless of how you feel.

DEVELOP AN ATTITUDE OF GRATITUDE

He who sacrifices thank-offerings honours Me, and he prepares the way that I may show him the salvation of God [Psalm 50:23].

A grateful heart is essential to understanding the wonders of your new life, and to growing in your relationship with God. You are surrounded with blessings—if you have eyes to see them. As you go through each day, take short breaks to give thanks for…

- o The Lord's overwhelming love for you
- o What Jesus has done for you
- o The blessings of the day
- o The people God has given you

- Health, shelter, clothing, food
- Anything else you can think of!

You'll be amazed at the difference it makes to you.

READ THE WORD 1

To grow in your relationship with God, you need to know what He is like.

> *The Son is the radiance of God's glory and the exact representation of His being [Hebrews 1:3].*

Jesus came to reveal God to you. And you will find out about Him by studying the Bible, which is also known as 'the Scriptures' or the 'Word of God'. The Bible is a collection of books, and the books which particularly paint a picture of Jesus, are known as the Gospels: Matthew, Mark, Luke and John. Whatever you see of Jesus in these books—His thoughts, words and deeds—that's what God is like.

One way of learning about God is as follows:

- Set aside some time daily. You will need a Bible, a pen and notebook.
- Find a peaceful spot and become quiet inside.
- Ask the Lord to come close and ask Him to show you things in His Word.
- Start with the book of Luke and read a chapter at a time, slowly and meditatively.

FUEL FOR THE JOURNEY 1

- o Reflect on what you have learned about Jesus. Then consider what this tells you about God the Father.
- o Talk to the Lord about what you have read, then spend some time quietly listening for His voice. Write down any thoughts and impressions which settle in your mind.

CHAPTER 9

THE POWER OF THE CROSS

WHY IS THE CROSS IMPORTANT?

The apostle Paul said that he preached 'nothing but Christ crucified' [1 Corinthians 2:2], so central was the Cross to his Gospel. And, for us as 'new creations', it is the basis on which our whole lives are founded. The Cross is not only the answer to our shortfall, it is the answer to every question, every problem faced by mankind, for Jesus took on Himself the sin and suffering of the whole world. If we are looking for internal peace, the Cross is the place to start.

Isaiah 53 is one of the most important chapters in the Bible. Hundreds of years before Christ, Isaiah had a prophetic revelation about what would be accomplished through the coming Messiah. It's essential to take time to grasp the enormity of what he was saying. Not only was Jesus to die so we would be forgiven our sin, and be healed spiritually; but also, to set us free from the consequences of living in a fallen world: physically, mentally and emotionally.

Many are deeply wounded as a result of other people's actions, and many struggle with mental or physical health issues, as well as with guilt and shame (which will be explored in more detail in the next chapter). All these things which work 'death' in us are the result of the activity of the satanic 'Prince of this world' [John 12:31], and the very real forces of darkness.

However, Jesus came to wage war and set people free from every sort of bondage.

> *The reason the Son of God appeared was to destroy the devil's work [1 John 3:8].*

We see that battle being fought in every healing, every deliverance, and every restoration during Jesus' ministry. However, the final victory over the Evil One's destruction was won on the Cross [John 16:11] and is described by Isaiah in the passage below.

ISAIAH CHAPTER 53

Alternative translations of the original Hebrew text are given in brackets, to amplify and increase our understanding of that amazing event:

> *Who has believed our message, and to whom has the arm of the Lord been revealed? He grew up before Him like a tender shoot, and like a root out of dry ground. He had no beauty or majesty to attract us to Him, nothing in His appearance that we should desire Him.*
>
> *He was despised and rejected by mankind, a man of (physical and mental) sorrows, and familiar with suffering (sickness and disease). Like one from whom people hide their faces, He was despised, and we held Him in low*

esteem. Surely He took up (removed to a distance, like the scapegoat) our ('our' is emphatic) infirmities (sicknesses) and carried our sorrows (physical, emotional and mental pain), yet we considered Him punished by God, stricken (a word used in connection with leprosy) by Him, and afflicted.

But He was pierced (defiled) for our transgressions (rebellion), He was crushed for our iniquities (punishment); the punishment that brought us peace (well-being, wholeness, safety, prosperity, peace with God and man) was on Him, and by His wounds we are healed. (Literally, 'by the means of His stripes there is healing for us'.)

We all, like sheep, have gone astray, each of us has turned to our own way; and the Lord has laid on Him the iniquity of us all. He was oppressed and afflicted (humiliated), yet He did not open His mouth; He was led like a lamb to the slaughter, and as a sheep before its shearers is silent, so He did not open His mouth.

By oppression and judgement He was taken away. Yet who of His generation protested? For He was cut off from the land of the living; for the transgression of My people He was punished. He was assigned a grave with the wicked, and with the rich in His death, though He had done no violence, nor was any deceit in His mouth.

Yet it was the Lord's will to crush Him (break Him in pieces) and cause Him to suffer (make weak, sick or diseased), and though the Lord makes His life an offering for sin, He will see His offspring and prolong His days, and the will of the Lord will prosper in His hand.

THE POWER OF THE CROSS

After He has suffered, He will see the light of life (fruit of His suffering) and be satisfied; by His knowledge (or, by knowledge of Him) My righteous servant will justify (declare righteous) many, and He will bear (carry away to a distance) their iniquities.

Therefore, I will give Him a portion among the great, and He will divide the spoils with the strong, because He poured out His life unto death, and was numbered with the transgressors. For He bore the sin of many (for the rebellious ones He interposed, came between them and their punishment), and made intercession for the transgressors.[1]

Have you felt…

- spurned and rejected
- weighed down with sorrow or grief
- ignored, despised and of no account
- wrongly accused or humiliated

- oppressed and broken
- stressed, anxious or fearful
- isolated or far from God
- physically or mentally tested

- beleaguered with sickness and disease
- physically, emotionally or mentally wounded
- guilt-ridden or shamed
- lacking in peace

Jesus took it all upon Himself on the cross; He died to set you free.

In Genesis, we read that the Lord rested after completing the work of creation [Genesis 2:2-3]. As Adam and Eve were created on the last day of this process, their first day was a day of rest—resting in the finished work of the Creator.

In John 19:30, we read that at the point of death, Jesus cried out, 'It is finished!' He had completed His task; He had taken the judgement on Himself for every single thing which works devastation in mankind. Then He bowed His head (literally 'rested') and died; the Greek construction signifying that He deliberately put His head into a position of rest before death.

The Father rested after completing the work of creation; Jesus rested after completing His work of redemption; and we, His new creation, receive internal peace and well-being, by laying down the human drive to work things out on our own, and resting in His finished work.

RHYTHMS OF GRACE

HEAR AND RESPOND to the voice of God

Become really quiet inside. Turn your heart of affection towards the Lord and ask Him to speak.

Whatever you are grappling with, bring it to the Cross right now. In your imagination, lay it down before Him.

THE POWER OF THE CROSS

RECEIVE His wonderful provision

Lord Jesus, I believe You died for my sake, to set me free. Thank You for taking my burden of _____ so I would not have to carry it anymore. I lay it down before You and receive the grace of freedom.

Thank You that You have heard my prayer, and I'm receiving freedom from my burden right now. Amen

GOING DEEPER: PERSONAL OR GROUP STUDY

1. Read Isaiah 53 through several times. List the different human ailments that Jesus suffered when He was crucified. Which of these conditions can you identify in your own life?

2. Spend some time before the Cross in your imagination, and picture Jesus taking on Himself your particular concerns. Thank Him that He bore all these things, so you wouldn't have to. Then be at rest!

If doing this as part of a group, consider laying a roughly made cross in the centre of the room. Each person could write down their personal issues, then in turn, pin their folded papers to the cross. They don't need to be shared with the group unless the group members are comfortable doing so. Pray together in pairs, declaring the freedom purchased by Jesus, over each other, with thanksgiving.

3. Read the excellent booklet, *The Divine Exchange* by Derek Prince,[2] available as a free PDF download from https://www.derekprince.org, or from various booksellers. There is a link on *'The Power of the Cross'* webpage.

Alternatively watch the YouTube video on the webpage, *The Exchange at the Cross*.[3]

What else have you learned about what Jesus achieved on the cross?

4. Reinforce what you have discovered through daily *Reflections on the Cross*, or take a personal 'retreat', available as

a digital magazine, to focus on how the *7 Wounds of Jesus* set us free. These resources are accessed from The *Power of the Cross* page on the website.

END NOTES

[1] Original text, NIVUK (see copyright page); amplification in brackets, my own.

[2] Derek Prince, (2020) *The Divine Exchange*, DPM-UK

[3] https://youtu.be/ooHwUHikehg

CHAPTER 10

MISSING THE MARK: OVERCOMING GUILT AND SHAME

> *And we all, who with unveiled faces contemplate the Lord's glory, are being transformed into His image with ever-increasing glory, which comes from the Lord, who is the Spirit [2 Corinthians 3:18].*

HELP! I'M FALLING SHORT

We live in a world where there is enormous pressure to measure up to the expectations placed upon us by family members, schools, workplaces, local churches, and a host of others (including ourselves)—all egged on by media advertising. The stress of these ambitions often produces, at best, a loss of personal well-being, and at worst, mental and physical illness. With the failure to measure up, both perceived and actual, comes guilt, shame and anxiety, yet still the aspiration lurks enticingly in the subconscious. We need to find peace in the midst of it all...

STANDARDS OF PERFECTION

We are also surrounded by images of perfection; flawless appearance, family-relationships, home décor or food-choice—whatever it is, there's a glowing picture of it somewhere. And alongside the visual imagery we have the self-help gurus who insist we can have it all if we follow their example. We are told the perfect man or woman is fit and well-toned, eats a bewildering array of 'life-giving' foods, in addition to a rich variety of supplements with exotic names. They hold down high-powered jobs, parent the rising stars of tomorrow, are well-travelled and well-read, have interesting hobbies, masses of friends and still find time for voluntary work!

And we are led to believe we too can have this perfection if we will only follow these five steps or buy that product. The sense of inadequacy these images of perfection engender in ordinary mortals either produces frenetic activity, or a rush to the comfort of the biscuit tin.

DEMANDS OF THE WORKPLACE

The idea of perfection also features strongly in the realm of employment, only there it masquerades as 'excellence'. If we will only work harder, faster or smarter, we too will make super-employee status with all its benefits. And many of us try, working long hours to achieve targets, only to find, somewhere along the way, the goal posts have moved yet again. And if we are, by chance, one of the fortunate few who have measured up for a while, and ticked all the boxes, then we live with the stress of trying to maintain that exalted place. Reproach hangs over the workplace, ready to settle on those found wanting.

CHURCH EXPERIENCE

It is often no better in the church. If you love Jesus, there is frequently an expectation that you will show your commitment by serving more, supporting this or that programme or ministry, and, of course, attending every meeting. Add to that Bible studies and prayer groups, conferences and special events, no wonder the way to Heaven is littered with exhausted Christians.

SIN

And then there's the guilt which comes from the unfashionable word 'sin', which in modern idiom masquerades as bad habits, weaknesses and negative tendencies. Whether we describe it as 'sin' or not, our habits of over-eating, bad temper, dishonesty, cheating, one-upmanship, or whatever, bring shame on us, a shame that gnaws at our inner being.

In addition, there's the guilt which comes from omission—the host of things we think we could have done or should have done. This guilt can be harder to shift as it is often non-specific, just a general sense of having fallen short.

In all these things we wear reproach like a garment:

reproach from people around us, and our reproach of ourselves. We have that sense of having been found wanting, and either fall into depression, or ramp ourselves up for another attempt. Where there is reproach, there is no rest.

BORN FOR GLORY

We know inwardly that we were born for something better than this [Hebrews 2:10]. The Bible pinpoints this condition, saying:

> *...for all have sinned and fall short of the glory of God [Romans 3:23].*

But it doesn't just point a finger, it offers the ultimate solution.

The truth is, there is only one who is perfect or excellent, and that is God. In the human heart there is a subconscious understanding, a vision of the God of glory, and the perception that man was originally designed to live in that glory with Him. Our efforts after perfection are attempts to regain that place.

But man's innate shortfall stands in the way. No one can get anywhere close to the glory of God.

JESUS BRIDGED THE GAP

Enter Jesus…

Jesus came to bridge the gap. He came to show us what

it was supposed to be like: a sinless man walking in harmony with a holy God. When He was crucified, He took the judgement for our shortfall, by taking all our guilt and failures on Himself. Dying naked, viewed by disappointed followers, and jeering crowds, He knew all about shame and reproach. And He endured all this, so we could be free.

And so we step into rest by acknowledging our state. We have to put down our pride, and admit we have been found wanting, that we can't do it on our own. This admission isn't just something we do to enter the Christian life, then once safely in, go back to our own efforts at living. This must be our lifestyle from now on: we haven't got what it takes—and it's ok!

Acknowledging our state of failure will take us into despair, unless we add the second step, which is to trust that Jesus bridged the gap through His death on the cross. He has already paid the price for our failures, so we can be free. We don't need to *earn* anything; He has done it all.

Jesus calls us to live in the glory with Him, to fill us with Himself. Responding is a no-brainer; we get to exchange our stress, our guilt, our sense of shame and reproach for His peace. That wholeness and freedom from failure is known in the Bible as 'righteousness'. But rather than a list of 'oughts' or rules for living, New Testament righteousness is a *gift* from the Father purchased through Jesus' sacrifice, which we can do nothing to merit. He took all our failures, so we could have *His* righteousness [2 Corinthians 5:21].

It's out of that place of completeness and freedom that we can live a new life; and that new life, rather than being externally imposed, can flow from the inside-out.

> *And we all, who with unveiled faces contemplate the Lord's glory, are being transformed into his image with ever-increasing glory, which comes from the Lord, who is the Spirit. [2 Corinthians 3:18]*

We get to live in the glory, after all.

RHYTHMS OF GRACE

RECEIVE His wonderful provision

Get really quiet inside.

Centre your heart on God, and listen…

Then pray:

> *Lord Jesus, I know how much I continually miss the mark, and that I often wear reproach like a garment. I cannot measure up to the standards of perfection that surround me, however hard I try. I ask You to forgive me, and cleanse me from all my shortfall.*
>
> *Lord Jesus, You came to fill the gap; thank You for having already paid the price for my sin and my failures:*

- *Everything I shouldn't have done, but did anyway*
- *Everything I could have done but didn't*
- *Every wrong choice and decision*
- *Every wrong thought, wrong speech and wrong action*
- *Every failure in self-discipline*
- *Every failure to meet expectations and measure up*
- *Every bit of poor-quality work*
- *Every bit of guilt and shame*
- *Every failed attempt to be perfect*
- *Every…*

You received all the judgement for my failures in Your body, so that I can stand complete and whole before the Father; and You washed me clean by shedding Your blood, so my conscience can be completely clear.

I choose to trust in Your provision. I exchange my failure for your righteousness, and my stress, guilt and reproach for Your peace. Come Lord and fill me with Your glory!

Put out your hands and receive from Him right now.

MISSING THE MARK: OVERCOMING GUILT AND SHAME

GET IN THE FLOW of His Spirit

Speak out your gratitude for what He has done. The more you vocalise it, the more gratitude and joy will rise up and overflow.

GIVE FREELY because you are blessed

Enjoying a new freedom from guilt, shame and anxiety? Why not share your experience of God's grace?

GOING DEEPER: PERSONAL OR GROUP STUDY

1. Look for images of 'perfection' in the media this week. What do you have to do to achieve that glorified state? How do these adverts make you feel? (If doing this as part of a group study, perhaps collect appropriate images for a discussion.)

2. Are you happy with the way you look? Does this have any effect on your everyday life?

3. Reflect on your workplace culture: is working with a 'spirit of excellence' rewarded, or only 'excellence as a destination'? How much pressure do you feel to achieve, or maintain an achievement? How do you respond to this?

4. What about church culture? Do you feel measured as a Christian by the amount you are involved in a church programme, or by the intensity of your devotional life? How do you respond to the expectations of other Christians?

5. Which sins or shortcomings make you feel like you're falling short? Who do you feel reproached by?

- God?
- Yourself?
- Family members?
- Other Christians?
- Employers or colleagues?

6. What happened to man's original destiny? What is God's solution to the problem of falling short, and how do we avail ourselves of this solution? What exchange will be made?

7. Take time now to be quiet before the Lord and pray through the prayer in the Rhythms of Grace section of this chapter.

(It may help to make a list of everything that's causing you to miss the mark; then pin it to a simple cross made from two pieces of wood while you pray. A physical action demonstrating a spiritual truth often has a powerful effect.)

Losing guilt and shame can have a transformational effect in your life. Write and tell me how you get on at journeyintorest@gmail.com

CHAPTER 11

FUEL FOR THE JOURNEY 2

Some more life-giving habits to foster:

PRACTISE THE PRESENCE

When you get up in the morning, and before you go to sleep at night, spend some time in the Lord's presence. Then develop this, so you take 5-minute snatches throughout the day.

- o Become very quiet inside

- o Turn your heart of affection towards Him and ask Him to come close

- o Speak out your love for Him

- o Ask Him to refill you with Himself

READ THE WORD 2

> *For the word of God is alive and active. Sharper than any double-edged sword, it penetrates even to dividing soul and spirit, joints and marrow; it judges the thoughts and attitudes of the heart [Hebrews 4:12].*

Another reason for reading the Bible (*See Fuel for the Journey 1*) is so that you can re-align yourself with God. In fact, the basic meaning of the Greek word for 'repentance', used in the New Testament, is to 'change your way of thinking'. Aligning our thinking, speaking and behaviour with God's word is the secret of powerful Christian living.

Continue with your Bible reading: after the book of Luke, read the other Gospels, followed by the Book of Acts. You may find it helpful to journal your reflections.

- What illumination have you had? What have you learned about Jesus, God the Father, or the Holy Spirit?

- What have you learned about the way different types of people in the Bible responded to Jesus? Do they remind you of anyone? Can you identify with any of them?

- Does the passage challenge you? In what way? What action are you going to take?

- Have you any questions? Is there anything you don't understand? How are you going to find trustworthy answers to your queries?

- Talk to the Lord about what you have read.

PRAYER

All relationships need communication to thrive, and prayer is essentially a conversation with a beloved friend. It is talking to God in your everyday language and listening to His response. It doesn't require a prayer book, or specially composed prayers, just a desire to seek Him out.

Hearing God talk back takes practice, like learning to tune a radio to an air frequency. You may hear His voice through your Bible reading: a particular verse may 'jump out at you'; something someone says may really strike you; or it may be a thought, impression or picture in your mind. The acid test of hearing correctly (is it me or is it God?), is whether what you have heard agrees with Scripture. If it doesn't—it's not God.

Talk to Him throughout your waking hours, as you would to a beloved friend, sharing the issues and delights of the day, and asking for His input.

As well as frequent communication, close relationships also need dedicated quality time. Set some specific time aside to spend with the Lord.

- Find a peaceful spot and become really quiet inside.

- Ask the Lord to come close. Thank Him for His presence.

- Tell Him about your needs and concerns, and those of the people around you.

o   Listen for His answers.

DECLARATIONS

As well as aligning our thinking with God's thoughts, it is really important to change the way we talk to reflect His truth. The reasons for this are explained in Chapter 20, *The Power of the Spoken Word*, but until then, do take time to regularly verbalise any declarations suggested. In addition, there are many pages on the website which have PDF files to download, which contain relevant affirmations.

CHAPTER 12

GOD'S PROMISE OF PROVISION

My God will supply all your needs according to His riches in glory in Christ Jesus [Philippians 4:10 NASB].

Children of rich parents have a certain sort of 'rest' because they know their parents have the ability to extricate them from many difficulties and smooth their way generally. How much more can we, the children of God, rest in His amazing promise of provision for us...

RESTING IN THE FINISHED WORK OF GOD

Biblical rest is about resting in the finished work of God. The Lord's last work of creation was to make man. Then He rested. Man's first day, therefore, was a day of rest—a rest in the finished work of God.

THE FIGHT FOR A FRUITFUL LIFE

Everything Adam and Eve needed was in the garden for them; their commission was to take and develop it all. When they fell (rebelled against God), there was a penalty for both them and the ground. No longer could they receive everything they needed freely from the Lord's hand, instead they would have to sweat to wrest their living from the earth. No longer would their labour have the blessing of God upon it; they would have to fight for fruitfulness against thorns and thistles. And this was the inheritance they passed on to their descendants.

THE PROMISED LAND: THE PLACE OF SUPERNATURAL PROVISION

This state was portrayed graphically by the enslavement of the nation of Israel in Egypt, where the land was irrigated by hand, the epitome of fruitfulness borne out of heavy labour. After a dramatic deliverance from Egypt, the Israelites were promised a home of their own, in a land irrigated by rain from Heaven, a land flowing with 'milk and honey' [Deuteronomy 11:19-12].

They would inherit a land filled with houses they didn't build, wells they didn't dig, and vineyards and olive groves they didn't plant [Deuteronomy 6:3; 10-12]—echoes of the provision for Adam. It was described as a place of rest. Not a place of inactivity, but a place of supernatural provision, which they were to develop, and from which they were to bless the world.

After the Fall, God's plan of redemption was immediately put into action. The rest Israel was to experience in the Promised Land was a shadow of the real thing, fulfilled in Jesus.

REDEEMED FROM STRIVING

We see in Jesus, a man at rest, a man who lived with complete awareness of His Father's provision, at all times. It wasn't the rest of inactivity, but the rest of a man who, in the middle of the pressing needs of humanity, was utterly unhurried. He never worried or fretted; whether it was provision for His own needs, a miracle of healing for the sick, or wisdom in the face of accusations, Jesus always received from the Father's hand all that He needed. And in doing so, He showed us how man was designed to live.

When Jesus died on the cross, He dealt with every curse that had fallen on mankind, in order to return us to that original design [Galatians 3:13]. In the Garden of Gethsemane, we read He sweated great drops of blood, as He wrestled with the labour that lay ahead of Him. That shed blood frees us from the yoke of slavery, from having to wrest our living from an unreceptive ground, and releases to us the unlimited resources of Heaven, the provision of God the Father.

Jesus also bled when the crown of thorns was rammed upon His head. Those terrible spikes recall the thorns and thistles which the ground would yield for Adam and his race [Genesis 3:17-19]. Through Jesus' shed blood, Adam's seed was redeemed from the curse of unfruitful labour and poverty, and the blessing of God was released on the work of their hands.

RESTING IN GOD'S PROMISE OF PROVISION

To rest involves humility: the giving up of toil, of control, and the giving of ourselves into the Lord's hands. To rest depends on faith: in choosing to trust and rely on the goodness of God and on the finished work of the Cross. Entering His rest changes everything. The book of Hebrews instructs us to labour to enter that truth [Hebrews 4:11]—to wrestle with the concept, like a dog with a bone, until we really get it.

And so, we enter God's rest with the understanding that Jesus has opened the way for us, to find in the Father everything we need for every eventuality—just like He did.

OUR FUTURE HOPE

At present, we live in a fallen world, and it's against this backdrop that we experience God's provision. And because living and walking in faith is a learning curve for us, we won't always access the fulness of God's supply in this life. Nonetheless, at those times we can be confident in His promise to never leave us or forsake us [Matthew 28:20; Hebrews 13:5], and that He will always work things for our eternal good [Romans 8:28].

In addition, whatever our circumstances, the Bible is clear there is an unassailable future hope provided for those who believe God [Revelations 21]; and before that time, the comfort of knowing we will be with Him after death [2 Corinthians 5:8; Philippians 1:21-23], along with other believers [Hebrews 12:22-24]. He wants everyone to access these promises—no exceptions—and has paid the necessary price to open up the way. The only requirement for any of us, is to receive what He is offering on the terms He has laid out, through the 'open door' of Jesus [John 14:6].

RHYTHMS OF GRACE

HEAR AND RESPOND to the voice of God

- Get very quiet inside.

- Turn your heart towards the Lord and ask Him to speak.

- Listen to His voice.

RECEIVE His wonderful provision

Whatever your current circumstances, the Lord Jesus has promised to be with you in it.

Allow everything within to become still—including any anxious thoughts—then ask Him to come close. Turn your heart towards Him and allow His love, compassion and strength to wash over you.

GOD'S PROMISE OF PROVISION

GOING DEEPER: PERSONAL OR GROUP STUDY

1. In common language, what do people mean when they talk about 'rest'? How does biblical rest differ from this?

2. Read Genesis Chapters 1-2. Think about Adam and Eve exploring Eden on their first day; imagine their responses and write down as many words as you can to describe them. (If you are inspired, you could use these as a starting point for a creative project.)

3. One of the key things about the serpent's enticement, was that it got them to question the goodness of God. Ask the Lord to show you areas where you doubt His goodness. Confess them to Him and receive forgiveness. Then research what His Word says about your situation and declare His truth over your life.

4. What was the consequence of the Fall for mankind in terms of biblical rest? How was this consequence illustrated by the Egyptian regime? What was God's response?

5. Read the story of Israel's captivity, release, and entry into the Promised Land, in the books of Exodus chapters 1-15, and Joshua chapters 1-11. (Alternatively, read the account in a Children's Bible.) Make notes on anything which strikes you.

6. Why might we describe Jesus as a man of rest?

7. What happened to mankind's struggle and toil when Jesus died on the cross? What do we have to do, to enter the rest purchased by Jesus?

8. What impact does this all have on your life? Do you need to take action?

CHAPTER 13

EXPERIENCING GOD'S PRESENCE

My presence will go with you and I will give you rest.
[Exodus 33:14]

MAN'S ORIGINAL DESTINY

We read in Genesis that God created the earth in six days, and on the seventh, He rested. Man's first day was a day of rest. Not only was it a rest in the provision of God [see Genesis 1-2]—we can imagine Adam and Eve spending that first day exploring the Garden and revelling in all they found—but it was a rest in the manifest presence of God too. There is a beautiful snapshot in the account of the Lord God walking in the Garden, 'in the cool of the day' and looking for Adam and Eve to fellowship with them. Sadly, because of their rebellion, sin entered Paradise, and they could no longer walk freely with the Lord. Their intimate relationship with God was broken, and rest was forfeited.

We hear the tragic cry of their son Cain, after he murdered his brother:

EXPERIENCING GOD'S PRESENCE

> *Today You are driving me from the land, and I will be hidden from Your presence; I will be a restless wanderer on the earth, and whoever finds me will kill me [Genesis 4:14].*

GOD'S PLAN OF REDEMPTION

In these circumstances we find the starting point for the human malaise: restlessness, fear, toil, stress and anxiety.

The Lord however, in His foreknowledge, already had a plan of redemption. He was unwavering in His intent to have a people whom He could live amongst [Leviticus 26:11]. He chose the nation of Israel as His own, and manifested His presence among them in a pillar of cloud by day, and fire by night; in the tabernacle, which was pitched in the middle of the camp, and specifically over the Ark of the Covenant, which was carried before them into battle, and on their journeying. Later, we read that the glory of the Lord, which is one expression of the manifest presence of God, filled the magnificent temple which was built to house the Ark. And in the golden age of Solomon which followed, the Lord 'gave them rest from their enemies' [1 Chronicles 22:9].

This rest however, was largely the external rest of peace and prosperity. The internal condition was a different matter. For the majority of Israelites, the prospect of meeting God was a thing of terror, and the glory of the Lord was something to be marvelled at from a safe distance. There was only a handful of people who had any sort of intimate relationship with God, and knew the benefits of the pursuit of His presence in their personal lives.

JESUS: THE MANIFEST PRESENCE

Into this context came Jesus—God Himself revealed. God literally 'tabernacled' among us [John 1:14; the Greek word for dwelt, (skene) means 'to pitch a tent, or to tabernacle']. And His manifest presence became available to everyone who came into contact with Him—rich and poor, young and old, healthy and sick.

> *'Come to Me', Jesus said, 'all you who are weary and burdened and I will give you rest' [Matthew 11:28].*

And those who responded to Him received healing, deliverance, peace, forgiveness, love and acceptance. They received rest.

Jesus died so that the separation between the holy God and sinful man could be bridged, so that the Holy Spirit, who is God Himself, could come and invade every life which gives Him welcome. The presence of God is available to everyone who comes to Him through the open door created by the death and resurrection of Jesus.

We are to live with the awareness of the presence of God in us and around us. God's presence is, for us, coming 'home', it's where we were always meant to be. And one day, of course, we are promised that we will see Him face to face [Revelation 22:4].

Thou hast formed us for Thyself, and our hearts are restless until they find rest in Thee. [Augustine 397 AD][1]

THE HOLY SPIRIT: GOD'S PRESENCE IN OUR LIVES

When it was time for Jesus to return to the Father, He made His disciples a promise:

> *I will ask the Father, and He will give you another advocate, (helper, comforter) to help you and be with you forever—the Spirit of truth. The world cannot accept Him, because it neither sees Him nor knows Him. But you know Him, for He lives with you and will be in you. I will not leave you as orphans; I will come to you [John 14:17-18].*

RECOGNISING HIS PRESENCE

Science teaches us that there are radio signals constantly flowing around us, however we only hear the sounds those signals are making if we have a radio switched on, and tune in to the frequency correctly.

This is a physical picture of a spiritual truth: the earth is filled with the presence of God—but if we have accepted His invitation to come into relationship with Him, He actually chooses to take up residence in us. By our faith in the Lord Jesus, we have been 'switched on' to God; but then we need to learn to 'tune in' to His presence—and this takes practice.

TRY THESE STEPS

1. Give thanks throughout the day for the truth of His

presence with you:

> *Lord, thank You that according to Your Word, You are filling this room (or wherever you are) with Your presence. Thank You that through the Holy Spirit You also fill me with Yourself. Thank You for Your promise that You will never leave me or forsake me.*

2. Then take time at intervals during the day to really focus: Get very quiet inside and turn your 'heart of affection' towards the Lord.

Ask Him to help you *experience* His presence.

- Wait quietly, keeping the 'gaze of your heart' on Him—and listen. Write down or speak out the thoughts and impressions which come to mind.

- Finish by thanking Him for all He has done for you.

In the same way that our physical bodies react to external stimuli—heat, light or water, for example, people often report experiencing specific sensations when the Lord has 'come present' in a special way. Some sensations which have been described to me, include a feeling of deep internal silence or peace, shaking or trembling in the body, spontaneous laughter, tears welling up, a frisson of inner excitement, an intense emotional reaction to beauty, and intense feelings of joy, or of being loved.

Everyone is different, and you will react to the presence of God in your own unique way. It is really important that you value your own manner of response rather than comparing yourself with others. Don't worry if you don't feel anything at first—sometimes it takes time for our souls (where our emotions live) to catch up with the truth which has taken hold in our spirits; and it also takes time to recognise our own particular responses.

In addition, it is essential that we do not mistake sensation in ourselves or others, as evidence of a superior spirituality; a focus on 'manifestations' rather than the truth of Christ, has led many well-meaning Christians into error, and others into the distressing misconception that they have had an 'inferior' encounter with God.

RHYTHMS OF GRACE

RECEIVE His wonderful provision

First, we need to 'switch on to God' in order to experience His presence.

Re-read the chapters, *A Brand-New Life* and *The Holy Spirit and You*, if you need to. Then take the steps outlined above to learn to recognise the Lord's presence.

GIVE FREELY because you are blessed

As children of God, we are also to carry His presence in us

not just for our own benefit, but for the world around us. We can ask the Holy Spirit to fill us daily, and then cause His 'rivers of life' to flow out of us to touch everyone we meet. [John 7:38]

GOING DEEPER: PERSONAL OR GROUP STUDY

1. Does God want to be known and experienced by mankind? What makes you think so? How did we become separated from Him?

2. What was meant by 'rest' in the Old Testament? How was that concept expanded in the New Testament? Why do you think the presence of God brings rest?

3. Jesus brought the presence of God right into the nitty-gritty of people's lives. What effect did that have?

4. People can no longer experience God incarnate by encountering Him in the physical person of Jesus. But on the cross Jesus dealt with the separation between us and the Father, and then sent the Holy Spirit to live in us, and be with us, so we could live permanently in God's presence.

Take a few minutes now to turn your heart of affection towards the Lord and ask Him to come close. Ask Him to expand your awareness of His presence, and thank Him that He is close to you now.

What do you notice happening in your body?

- A feeling of peace or calmness?
- A frisson of joy or excitement?
- Burning, tingling, or shaking in your limbs?
- A desire to laugh or cry?

- Something else?

A person's body often responds in one of these ways to the Presence. However, there isn't a 'right' way, because everyone's different—how do *you* respond?

5. David wrote: 'I have set the Lord always before me' [Psalm 16:8,9].

Why not try…

- Taking short breaks throughout the day to turn your heart again towards God.

- Listening to instrumental worship music, and allow it to usher you into His presence.

- Turning your heart of affection towards Him before you go off to sleep at night.

- Making a journal of your experiences as you learn how to enter and enjoy God's presence. (If you are finding it difficult, do keep persevering; all new skills take time to learn!)

- Downloading the PDF *God is with Me* from *Experiencing God's Presence* page of the website, and start to declare these truths over your life.

6. Read the spiritual classic, *The Practice of the Presence of God* by Brother Lawrence (You can find details on the webpage).

EXPERIENCING GOD'S PRESENCE

Has anything you've read particularly struck you?

END NOTES

[1] Augustine of Hippo (397 AD) *Confessions Book 1*
[2] Brother Lawrence (1692) *The Practice of the Presence of God*

CHAPTER 14

PSALM 91

Afraid of the future? Read the Psalm which describes the power of experiencing God's presence and protection...

Whoever lives within the secret shadow of Shaddi, hidden in the strength of God Most High, will always be kept safe and feel secure!

Here's how I describe Him: He's the Hope that holds me, and the Stronghold to shelter me, The only God for me, and my Great Confidence.

Yes He will rescue you from every hidden trap of the enemy, and He will protect you from false accusation and any deadly curse, His massive arms are wrapped around you, protecting you.

You can run under His covering of majesty and hide, His faithfulness is a wrap-around shield keeping you from harm. You will never worry about an attack of demonic forces at night, nor have to fear a spirit of darkness coming against you.

Don't fear a thing! Whether by night or by day, demonic

PSALM 91

danger will not trouble you, nor the powers of evil launched against you.

For God will keep you safe and secure, they won't lay a hand on you! Even in a time of disaster with thousands and thousands being killed, you will remain unscathed and unharmed!

You will be a spectator as the wicked perish in judgment, for you will still be kept safe and secure!

When we live our lives within the shadow of the God Most High, our Secret Hiding Place, we will always be shielded from harm!

How then could evil prevail against us, or disease infect us? God will send His messengers - angels with special orders to protect you wherever you go, defending you from all harm.

If you walk into a trap, they'll be there for you and keep you from stumbling! You'll even walk unharmed among the fiercest powers of darkness, trampling every one of them beneath your feet!

For here is what the Lord has spoken to me: "Because you have chosen to be My great lover, I have chosen to greatly protect you. I will set you in a high place, safe and secure before My face, I will answer your cry for help every time you pray, and you will find and feel My presence, even in your time of pressure and trouble.

I will be Your glorious Hero and give you success! You will be satisfied with a full life, and with all that I do for you!

> *For you will feast your eyes on the fullness of My salvation, drinking deeply of me!"*
>
> *[Psalm 91, Passion Translation[1]]*

WORRIED AND ANXIOUS?

Peel (or pele) towers are a familiar sight in the borderlands between Scotland and England. In a historically turbulent area, these towers were built hundreds of years ago for protection, with walls several feet thick, and in an elevated position, for surveillance. When cross-border raids took place, local landowners would gather their families, and sometimes nearby communities, into these strongholds for protection. Many of these towers are still intact after centuries, a testament to the skill of the builders, and those charged with repelling invaders.

Seeing these bastions always reminds me of Psalm 91, and the beautiful picture it paints of the safe place we have to run to in troubled times. Why not take time right now to creep into our Lord's protection?

WHEN FEAR TAKES HOLD...

> *The weapons we fight with are not the weapons of the world. On the contrary, they have divine power to demolish strongholds [2 Corinthians 10:4].*

Sometimes—particularly in the middle of the night—fear and anxiety take hold, and we need to take extra steps to combat them. As well as learning to take shelter in the 'shadow of God' [Psalm 91:1], we have also been given powerful spiritual weapons to counter 'enemy attack'.

If you are having problems resting in the Lord's 'stronghold', try the following:

THE WORD

You are my refuge and my shield; I have put my hope in Your word [Psalm 119:114].

1. Get very quiet inside and turn the focus of your heart towards the Lord. Ask the Holy Spirit to bring to mind every issue, big and small, which is a source of stress at the moment. Write them all down, without stopping to analyse. Then lay them down before your Heavenly Father.

2. Using the words of Psalm 91, thank Him for His promises. (There is a personalised version of the psalm, on the website.)

3. Find out what the Word says about your situation; there are several online concordances to help (for example, www.biblegateway.com). Then begin to declare God's thoughts over your life and circumstances. You can find out more about the power of the spoken word and the need for creating new mindsets in the next section.

THE NAME

The name of the Lord is a fortified tower; the righteous run to it and are safe [Proverbs 18:10].

The Border magnates were served, and often feared, by the surrounding communities. If representatives came to a dependent household in the name of a particular lord, their demands were satisfied immediately; dissenters would not be tolerated. The 'name' gave the messengers power. All the power of the lord—to elevate, honour and bless, or to evict, demand, and destroy—was summed up in the name. Happy were those who had the lord's favour!

In the same way, the Name of Jesus represents all that He is: our all-powerful, all-loving, all-glorious Saviour, who came to destroy the works of the Evil One [1 John 3:8]. And His Name is our safe place, our tower of refuge. This is not dependent on whether we feel worthy or not. It is not something we can ever earn. We have His favour, not because of anything we have done, but because He has taken away our guilt and shame, has called us righteous, and has invited us to find sanctuary in Him.

Therefore, as well as being able to hide ourselves in the Lord's 'stronghold', and use His Word as a powerful offensive weapon, we also have the right to use His Name as a shield against the Evil One's onslaught. In the 'Name of the Lord' we can declare protection over ourselves and our loved ones.

PSALM 91

THE BLOOD

When Jericho was threatened by attack from Israel, the prostitute, Rahab, kept herself and her family safe by displaying a red cord in her window [[You can read the story in Joshua 2]; and the woman praised in Proverbs 31 walked secure in the knowledge that her family were 'clothed in scarlet' [v:21], both prophetic references to the saving blood of Jesus that was to come.

When Jesus poured out His blood on our behalf, He completely defeated every destructive power raised against us. Although that victory was won decisively on the Cross, it still has to be enforced in the nitty-gritty of our lives. One way of doing this is by appealing to the power of 'the Blood of Jesus'.

> *In Him we have redemption through His blood, the forgiveness of sins, in accordance with the riches of God's grace [Ephesians 1:7].*

[See also, Romans 5:9; Ephesians 2:13; Colossians 1:20; Hebrews 9:14; 10:19; 1 Peter 1:18-20]

We read that the saints… 'triumphed over him (the Evil One) by the blood of the Lamb and by the word of their testimony' [Revelations 12:11]; and we can do the same. However, in order for us to use this weapon effectively against an attack of the enemy, we need to know what Jesus' death has accomplished. (Why not set aside time with the Lord to reread the 'Power of the Cross' chapter and ask for fresh revelation?) And having discovered what Jesus' blood has purchased for us, we can learn from our Old Testament forebears by 'covering ourselves and our loved-ones with

His blood' in prayer.

In addition, every time we 'break bread' we proclaim the power of the Lord's death over our circumstances, and 'the new covenant in His blood' [1 Corinthians 11:25-26]. Each time we come to the Lord's Table, let's take the opportunity to make it a faith-filled declaration of His victory and protection.

PRAISE

The final powerful tool in our 'weapons of spiritual warfare' that I want to mention here, is praise. Read the account of Jehoshaphat's defeat of Moab and Ammon [2 Chronicles 20], noting that the King's first response to the threat was to 'turn his eyes on the Lord' and offer the situation to Him; and then it was to face his enemies with a heart full of praise.

'Give thanks to the Lord, for His love endures forever.'

As they began to sing and praise, the Lord set ambushes against the men of Ammon and Moab and Mount Seir who were invading Judah, and they were defeated. [2 Chronicles 20:21-22]

Why not take some time right now to follow Jehoshaphat's example. Turn your heart towards the Lord, lay all your concerns before Him, then begin to thank Him for all His blessings. We live in a fallen world where bad stuff happens, but God is good all the time, continually showers us with blessings, and promises never to leave us or forsake us [Hebrews 13:5]. We are told He is enthroned on, or inhabits, the praises of His people [Psalm 22:3 NASB];

and where He is enthroned anything can happen!

RHYTHMS OF GRACE

RECEIVE His wonderful provision

Read the psalm again, aloud, personalising it, substituting *I, me* and *my* where appropriate (or use the PDF on the website). Then pray it section by section, over yourself and your loved ones, daily.

GOING DEEPER: PERSONAL OR GROUP STUDY

1. Make a list of common anxieties and fears. Using concordances (online or hard copies) research biblical promises for each one. If working in a group or pair, share your findings. Take some time to speak out, and give thanks for, specific promises.

(Thank You, Lord for your promise that…)

2. What is the significance of the 'Name of Jesus'? How can it be used to combat fear and anxiety?

3. Review some of the things Jesus purchased for us through His death, (See 'The Power of the Cross' chapter). Then, take time to break bread (see Fuel for the Journey 3, in Chapter 18) and as you take the wine, give thanks for these gifts.

4. What does it mean to 'cover' ourselves or our loved ones with the 'blood of Jesus'?

5. We are showered with blessings. How many can you think of? Spend some time giving thanks.

6. Read the next chapter, *Notes on Fear*. Have these reflections changed your perspective? Ask the Holy Spirit to help you examine your own belief system; do you have any deeply-rooted ideas which make it difficult to trust God?

PSALM 91

Confess these difficulties to the Lord and ask Him to help you find solid ground to stand.

END NOTES

[1]This Scripture quotation is from The Passion Translation®. Copyright © 2017, 2018 by Passion & Fire Ministries, Inc. Used by permission. All rights reserved. ThePassionTranslation.com]

CHAPTER 15

FURTHER NOTES ON FEAR

Many people are dealing with fear; fear relating to the present pandemic and health issues, fear relating to family or finances; fear of the future. Perhaps you are one of them?

FINDING A PLACE TO STAND

In order to deal with fear, we need to root out the underlying convictions which give it oxygen. We desperately need the reassurance that God really is looking out for us, and that the biblical promises work. The problem is, we often believe it all in a general sense, but struggle when it is *my* life, *my* family which is on the rack, *my* faith which needs to work right now.

The problem of suffering is one that has occupied great minds throughout the centuries, and is something that people get very riled about, defending their pet theory. I don't pretend to have all the answers, and you may not agree with my conclusions—and that's alright. But we all need to come to a place where we can rest, so there is a solid foundation for our faith, and so I offer this perspective in the hope that it might be of help to some.

There have been many people around the world who

have pronounced that various natural disasters, or even the present pandemic, are God's judgement on the world's wickedness. In addition, there is often a subtext in films and books, as well as in common conversation, which attributes all suffering to God's will. We hear that He has 'taken people' because 'He needs them more than us', has afflicted people with illnesses because it is 'good for them', and 'disciplines us' by sending sorrow after blessing. The problem with these conceptions is that it doesn't leave us anywhere to place our faith. If we believe that it is God that is doing this to us, how can we pray in faith for deliverance? If things are going well, how can we believe they will continue? And how can we merit the deliverance we need?

I lived like this for many years. I believed that God is good, and God is love, and had bought into the idea that sometimes His goodness and love is expressed in a way I might not understand, like a parent disciplining a young child. And I still believe that. However, an over-emphasis on this perspective left me anxious that some 'discipline' was always about to come my way, because I was so aware of my own failings. In addition, it seemed like many basic needs went unmet, despite the biblical promises, because not being a 'super-Christian' (like my heroes in books), I somehow hadn't done enough—or the right things—for God to hear and answer. With that mindset, I developed the expectation that blessing had to be earned, one way or another, but would inevitably be followed by hardship, with the result that I struggled to trust the Lord to keep me or my family safe and our needs met, and fear found fertile ground.

These days my perspective has changed, and so has my life. I no longer have an undercurrent of fear gnawing away inside, and while some anxieties still worm their way in and disturb my peace, I have the tools to recognise and deal with them. There are almost certainly holes in my theology, as I have said, but I have found a place to plant my feet, in order to be free from fear, and put my trust in the God who loves us passionately.

God created a good world, and meant it to be a place of blessing, and grace, abundance, and beauty. There was no sickness or suffering in His creation, and it was to be filled with His presence. Mankind was to work in partnership with Him to steward and develop it. Then sin entered, and creation 'fell', and through man's choice came under the influence of the Evil One, as referenced by Jesus himself. And with that fall came all the evils we know: man's inhumanity to man (and beast), selfish ambition, death and sickness, decay and disaster.

The Old Testament gives the graphic story of the contaminating nature of sin, and its consequences in terms of direct and indirect judgement. The book of Job also reports on the consequences of living in a fallen world, where the Evil One operates. (Job is a huge subject, far too lengthy to delve into at this point.)

Written into God's creation were divine laws and principles, including that of sowing and reaping. These continued after the Fall, becoming a tool in the Evil One's hand to bring about the devastation he planned. Eventually man's sin and rebellion would reap what it sowed, both in terms of a final cleansing showdown, and a continual cause and effect. To put it in simple terms, we know that if someone smokes heavily for a lifetime, it is quite possible they will contract cancer[1]. This is a common outcome of that action, rather than God specifically 'doing it to them'. In the same way, man has abused the environment, for profit, for centuries, and we are reaping the consequences in terms of cataclysmic natural events. Again, these are the results of human selfishness, rather than the specific direct judgements of God.

JESUS IS THE EXACT REPRESENTATION OF THE FATHER

If we want to know what God thinks of the situations which face us personally, we need to look first at the response of Jesus to the people around Him, as He was the exact representation of the Father, and came to reveal Him to us [Hebrews 1:13, John 14:9].

Jesus was very clear that He thought the world was under the jurisdiction of the Evil One [John 12:21; 14:30; 16:21], and that His mission was to deliver it from that bondage, in addition to providing an escape route from the final judgement on sin. This was all achieved through His death and resurrection. But He also came to deliver individuals from their specific struggles.

And so we read…

> *We know that we are children of God, and that the whole world is under the control of the evil one [1 John 5:19].*
>
> *Now is the time for judgement on this world; now the prince of this world will be driven out [John 12:21].*
>
> *Having cancelled the charge of our legal indebtedness, which*

stood against us and condemned us; He has taken it away, nailing it to the cross. And having disarmed the powers and authorities, He made a public spectacle of them, triumphing over them by the cross [Colossians 2:14].

He has sent Me to proclaim freedom for the prisoners and recovery of sight for the blind, to set the oppressed free, to proclaim the year of the Lord's favour [Luke 4:18].

…how God anointed Jesus of Nazareth with the Holy Spirit and power, and how He went around doing good and healing all who were under the power of the devil, because God was with Him [Acts 10:38].

Therefore, there is now no condemnation for those who are in Christ Jesus, because through Christ Jesus the law of the Spirit who gives life has set you free from the law of sin and death [Romans 8:1-2].

We never read of Jesus telling people that sickness and poverty was God's will, He saw these things clearly as coming from the hand of the Evil One and worked to set people free. The only people Jesus spoke judgement against were the religious ones who showed no mercy, and those who refused the way out He was offering [Matthew 23:13-39; John 3:18]. We are living in a period of grace, that is, unmerited favour, before the final judgement which will finally rid God's creation of every bit of evil, and the results of the Fall—a judgement which comes out of God's great love for the work of His hands. And rather than wanting humanity to suffer the just penalties for sin, God wants every single person to be saved! Through Jesus, He has provided a way out… but not all will accept the invitation.

NOTES ON FEAR

What a tragedy!

LIVING WITH FAITH IN A FALLEN WORLD

In our day—and every age—there have been people who have taken it on themselves to declare terrible pronouncements of judgement over their fellows, even over whole nations! Their predictions should be questioned, coming as they so often do from harsh and self-righteous hearts. The only warning of judgement that we should ever give time to is one given in humility, mourning and brokenness; one that exalts Jesus the Deliverer, and acknowledges that we have *all* fallen short, both personally and as nations.

> *But the wisdom that comes from heaven is first of all pure; then peace-loving, considerate, submissive, full of mercy and good fruit, impartial and sincere. Peacemakers who sow in peace reap a harvest of righteousness [James 3:17-18].*

In the meantime, we live in a fallen world, as agents of the Kingdom of God, Jesus having left us with a commission to continue His work. And so we are to stand in partnership with Him against the devastation we see released in the earth by the Evil One, commanded to enforce the victory won by Him on the cross.

Will we always see that victory worked out? Not always, because we are all on a learning curve, learning to trust Him, work with Him and use the tools He has given us. But, if we are willing, every unsuccessful skirmish trains us for the next encounter.

The crucial thing is to keep on trusting Him, even when our endeavours fail—and sometimes when we don't understand. He loves us with an everlasting love, and we have three promises which will carry us through the hard times. He has promised to be with us in whatever we are facing [Matthew 28:20; Hebrews 13:5]; He has promised to work everything out for our ultimate good [Romans 8:28]. And we have the hope of an eternal future without suffering [Revelation 7:17].

Why is all this important? Because if we can get hold of the fact that whatever we are facing, God is not doing it to us, it's the result of living in a fallen world, we are then free to put our trust in Him, without a crisis of faith and impugning His character. He does not need to be persuaded to help us. He has already shown His willingness by coming to earth, living in our fallen world, experiencing our griefs and sorrows, and by submitting to the most terrible death on our behalf. Now He is inviting us to work with Him, to see His Kingdom being released in our circumstances.

If we see that we are trainee kingdom-enforcers, we can also get rid of the idea that it's our fault when we don't get the answers we seek, that we haven't prayed enough, given enough, or been good enough to deserve an answer. The truth is, none of us deserve any blessing from the Lord—even the super-Christians we admire. Grace is His undeserved favour, just because He loves us. That's all. He who gave up His Son on our behalf, will freely give us all things [Romans 8:32].

And if the issues we are facing are the result of our own sin, bad judgements or foolishness, we still need not despair.

NOTES ON FEAR

Christ has covered all our shortfall; we can take these things to the cross, receive His forgiveness and cleansing, and then be free to pray with faith for deliverance.

Whatever you are facing at the moment, our Lord's desire is that you run *to* Him, not away, and that you believe in His passionate love and compassion for you. He is a good and faithful Father who longs to pour out His grace and mercy—and the comfort of His presence—on you in your time of need.

END NOTES

[1] https://www.cancerresearchuk.org/health-professional/cancer-statistics/worldwide-cancer#heading-Two

CHAPTER 16

WHO AM I REALLY?

Answering the question of who we are is fundamental to internal rest. Uncertainty about personal identity results in low self-esteem and is a huge stress-producer.

WHERE DO I GET MY SENSE OF SELF FROM?

Many people get their sense of self-worth from what they do, from their talents or their occupations. If circumstances change, and they can no longer utilise their skill or do their job, their sense of self can crumble. Others find their identity in the role they play as parents, children or carers. But children leave home, and parents or dependents die or move on, again often causing identity issues. And in the church, some find their raison d'être in ministry, but a change in location, or in church staffing often means starting again to establish a place to serve.

The stuff of life—both the common and the extraordinary—can have catastrophic effects on the lives of those whose sense of self are bound up in externals; casualties become lost, adrift and despairing, like ships without a rudder. The question of who we are goes right to

WHO AM I REALLY?

the very heart of man. We have to have a satisfying answer.

THE ANSWER TO MY PERSONAL IDENTITY STARTS IN GOD

The answer to who I am is found, not in myself or in what I do, but in God; and it begins—maybe surprisingly—with thinking rightly about Him. For many, the internal image of God is of a stern judge, aloof and unmoved, dispensing cold justice and discipline like a Victorian father.

If we want to know what He is really like, let's look at Jesus:

Then Jesus cried out... 'The one who looks at Me is seeing the One who sent Me' [John 12:45].

The Gospels show Jesus as accessible, intimate, compassionate, and overflowing with love and joy; the kind of man adults and children wanted to be around. The only people to whom Jesus showed Himself severe, were those who were self-righteous, self-contained, and thought they had need of nothing.

The Son is the radiance of God's glory and the exact representation of His being [Hebrews 1:3].

This is the God who says to us:

'I have loved you with an everlasting love!' [Jeremiah 31:3].

GOD SEES ME!

Am I just a face in the crowd, or a unique individual with a specific calling and destiny?

There is a basic human need to be seen and heard; to feel our lives have significance and purpose.

The good news is that God knows me completely, every thought, every action, every hope and every dream. And what is more, because He knows the end from the beginning, nothing I do will ever surprise or disappoint Him. And yet I am totally accepted...

PSALM 139

You have searched me, Lord, and You know me. You know when I sit and when I rise; You perceive my thoughts from afar.

You discern my going out and my lying down; You are familiar with all my ways. Before a word is on my tongue You, Lord, know it completely.

You hem me in behind and before, and You lay your hand upon me. Such knowledge is too wonderful for me, too lofty for me to attain.

Where can I go from Your Spirit? Where can I flee from Your presence? If I go up to the heavens, You are there; if I make my bed in the depths, You are there.

WHO AM I REALLY?

If I rise on the wings of the dawn, if I settle on the far side of the sea, even there Your hand will guide me, Your right hand will hold me fast.

If I say, 'Surely the darkness will hide me and the light become night around me,' even the darkness will not be dark to You; the night will shine like the day, for darkness is as light to You.

For You created my inmost being; You knit me together in my mother's womb. I praise You because I am fearfully and wonderfully made;

Your works are wonderful, I know that full well. My frame was not hidden from You when I was made in the secret place, when I was woven together in the depths of the earth.

Your eyes saw my unformed body; all the days ordained for me were written in your book before one of them came to be.

How precious to me are Your thoughts, God! How vast is the sum of them!

WHAT DOES GOD THINK OF ME?

From time to time there are news reports of personal belongings fetching thousands of pounds at auction because they belonged to someone famous; conversely, in times of depression, the value of real estate can sharply drop in price. Both illustrate the important truth that the worth of any item is totally dependent on what someone is willing to pay for it.

Jesus said:

> *Greater love has no one than this: to lay down one's life for one's friends [John 15:13].*

Jesus went through terrible suffering, laying down His life on the cross, because He thought you and I were worth paying the ultimate price for. Whatever circumstances may have suggested, or others may have told you, that is God's estimate of your worth—and don't let anyone tell you otherwise.

Not only do you have incredible value to God, you were chosen before the foundation of the world to become His child and a member of His family.

Take a look at these Scriptures:

> *For God so loved the world that He gave His one and only Son, that whoever believes in Him shall not perish but have eternal life [John 3:16].*

> *For He chose us in Him before the creation of the world to be holy and blameless in His sight. In love He predestined us for adoption to sonship through Jesus Christ, in accordance with His pleasure and will--to the praise of His glorious grace, which He has freely given us in the One He loves. In Him, we have redemption through His blood, the forgiveness of sins, in accordance with the riches of God's grace that He lavished on us, with all wisdom and understanding [Ephesians 1:4-8].*

WHO AM I REALLY?

> *But we do see Jesus, who was made lower than the angels for a little while, now crowned with glory and honour because He suffered death, so that by the grace of God He might taste death for everyone. In bringing many sons and daughters to glory, it was fitting that God, for whom and through whom everything exists, should make the pioneer of their salvation perfect through what He suffered. Both the one who makes people holy and those who are made holy are of the same family. So Jesus is not ashamed to call them brothers and sisters [Hebrews 2:9-11].*

Through faith in Jesus, we have become children of God, and our Father in Heaven delights in us. There is nothing we can do to make Him love us more than He does right now; there is nothing we can do to make Him love us less.

YOUR TRUE IDENTITY

Your true identity is that you are a cleaned up, forgiven, restored, empowered, beloved son or daughter of God, who is clothed in His righteousness—and everything you do comes from this knowledge.

RHYTHMS OF GRACE

RECEIVE His wonderful provision

Spend some time alone and become really quiet inside. Take some time to 'visit' the crucifixion in your imagination: see the baying crowds, the vicious lash, the shame and nakedness, the exhaustion, the barbarous nails, the scorn and derision, the agonising pain…

Then receive the amazing truth that it was all for you. He thought you were worth it all. Begin to thank Him.

Go on to thank Him for the following truths—declaring them aloud:

- Jesus thought I was worth dying for.

- God knows every detail about me, and He still loves me.

- When God looks at me, He doesn't see my imperfections…. He sees Jesus, and He says, 'This is My beloved child in whom I am well pleased.'

- My Father in Heaven delights in me.

- I am loved with an everlasting love.

- God is good all the time. God is good to me all the time.

- Nothing I can do will make Him love me more than He does at this moment.

- Nothing I can do will make Him love me less.

- I was chosen before the world was made, to be His child.

WHO AM I REALLY?

- My identity comes from who I am, not from what I do.
- I am the beloved son/daughter of God.

GOING DEEPER: PERSONAL OR GROUP STUDY

1. What are some of the things people look to for their sense of self or identity? Can you think of any others? What do you get your identity from?

2. In our search for identity, why is it important to think rightly about God?

3. If Jesus is the exact representation of God, what is He like?

4. What does God know about you (Psalm 139)? And knowing you, what is His plan for you?

5. What is your true identity? Declare God's truth about yourself aloud every day this week. There is a PDF on the website to help.

6. Read *He Loves Me! Learning to Live in the Father's Affection*[1] by Wayne Jacobsen. Has this book made any difference to your understanding? In the light of your studies so far, do you agree with his conclusions in chapter 12?

7. Poor or inadequate fathering leaves deep wounds in our identity. *I am Your Father: What Every Heart Needs to Know* by Mark Stibbe[2] addresses this issue, exploring what he

describes as 'the orphan heart', and points us to the healing available through our Heavenly Father's embrace.

END NOTES

[1] Wayne Jacobsen, (2008) *He Loves Me! Learning to Live in the Father's Affection*, FaithWords; 2nd edition

[2] Mark Stibbe, (2010) *I am Your Father: What Every Heart Needs to Know*, Monarch Books

CHAPTER 17

WHERE DO WE COME FROM?

In order to build a strong sense of self and personal identity, not only do we have to know *who we are*, the focus of the previous chapter, we also need to know *where we come from*—our place in the big picture.[1]

From Genesis to Revelation, the message is clear; the Bible is unequivocal about our origins:

- Genesis 1:1-3
- Job 38:4-7
- Psalm 139:13-16
- Isaiah 40:25-28
- Isaiah 45:12
- Isaiah 45:18
- Mark 10:5-9
- John 1:10
- Ephesians 3:9
- Revelation 4:11

The universe was created by God and is held together by Him.

For in Him all things were created: things in heaven and

> *on earth, visible and invisible, whether thrones or powers or rulers or authorities; all things were created by Him and for Him. He is before all things, and in Him all things hold together [Colossians 1:16].*

CREATED ON PURPOSE

That our origins are in deliberate design, rather than chance, is also displayed plainly throughout the universe.

We look at the order, symmetry, mathematical precision, and design in the natural world, and it all points to a Skilled Architect. We look at the breath-taking beauty, splendour and glory in the landscape, and wonder at the work of an Inspired Artist. We look at the minute detail invested in every living thing, and how everything fits together, and see evidence of an Intelligent Designer. We ignore these things at our peril. Belief in God as Creator is not an optional extra.

Romans 1:18-32 clearly teaches that God reveals Himself through nature. And it suggests that the refusal to recognise the Lord in creation, and give thanks to Him as Creator, unleashes consequences which have far-reaching results in society.

The last century has seen an unprecedented turning away from the belief in God as Creator, even among professing Christians. I believe this has had major consequences for the spiritual climate of our countries.

It's beyond the scope of this book to examine the theories of origin by chance, and compare them with arguments for creation, because although I am convinced by the latter, the Bible clearly teaches it is primarily a faith issue rather than an intellectual one.

> *By faith, we understand that the universe was formed at God's command, so that what is seen was not made out of what was visible [Hebrews 11:3].*

And a belief in creation as a deliberate act was clearly held by Jesus, the Word of God [Mark 10:6; 13:19].

WHY IS A BELIEF IN GOD AS CREATOR IMPORTANT?

Creation reveals something of the nature and glory of God. If we are tuned in, it is one of the means by which we can constantly be aware of His presence around us and learn more about Him and His ways. Although the natural world—like mankind—bears the consequences of the Fall, marring the image of God, His creation still fills our lives with blessings if we take time to notice. And our proper response of gratitude and thanksgiving is the path to joy.

If God is Creator, then the universe belongs to Him. He has a right to determine the laws and principles on which it runs, and the consequences when those laws are broken. If He is the God of all creation, we must respond to Him—ignoring Him is not an option.

Our present environmental crisis proclaims that we live on a despoiled planet. Mankind has rebelled against the Creator, and instead of stewarding the earth on behalf of our Maker, we have given place instead to the power of evil, causing sickness, death and destruction to be unleashed. But if God is Creator, then He is still ultimately in charge. He is working out His plan of redemption for His wayward planet and will have His way—this is the basis for the Gospel. And it is this which gives us hope and confidence in a dark and troubled world.

FOUNDATION FOR SELF-ESTEEM

If God is Creator, not one of us came about by chance, each was divinely purposed; therefore, our lives have meaning. And if God created us in His image, it means we were set apart from the animal kingdom, for the unique purpose of communing with the Almighty.

Knowing that we were created on purpose is essential to the sense of self; it's the foundation on which self-esteem is built. And what is more, the God of all creation knows every detail about us—and loves us passionately.

We read in Genesis, that the world was 'formless and void', God spoke, and it became something beautiful, filled with life. As God is the same yesterday, today and forever, this is the basis for our certainty that He can, and will, speak over the chaos of our lives and our sick world, and bring forth something amazing—if we let Him.

Having a correct theology is not enough, we need an encounter with the God whose Person is revealed in the works of His hands, and whose presence fills the universe. And there is only one appropriate response to that encounter: to bow before the Lord of all creation in thanksgiving, praise and worship. The Bible says that as the whole of the universe is lifting its voice in a song of praise, how can we then be silent?

Holy, holy, holy is the Lord Almighty; the whole earth is full of His glory [Isaiah 6:3].

MEET THE MAKER...

How do we move from right belief to experience?

If you have never encountered God as Creator before, and don't know where to start, here are some suggestions:

DEVELOP AN AWARENESS OF NATURE

Making use of all your senses...

- o Start to notice details in the natural world: textures and patterns, or sounds and scents, such as emerging leaf-buds, cloud-formation, birdsong or wayside flowers.

- o Keep a scrapbook, journal, thanksgiving diary, photo or video record of the passing seasons.

- o Choose a special spot, bench, window or skylight, and record what you see, and how things change over a period.

- o Become a sky or weather-watcher.

- o Notice people—made in God's image: their gifts, personality, appearance, and uniqueness.

WHERE DO WE COME FROM?

- Take a sensory walk once a week.

Use your observations as a focus for thanksgiving and praise.

SPEND TIME OUTDOORS

Set aside time regularly to get out into the 'natural world': the countryside, coast, local park or garden.

- Start by thanking God that His presence is filling the place. (This is true whether you 'feel' it or not.)

- Develop an expectation that you will have an encounter with God our Creator.

- Ask Him to reveal Himself to you.

- Become really still and start to use your senses. Give thanks for all that you notice.

Listening to God's voice takes practice—rather like tuning into a radio frequency—you will find thoughts and impressions start to form, but they may be a bit 'fuzzy' at first; stick with it, and they will become clearer.

UNABLE TO GET OUTSIDE?

- Have an encounter with God through photographs or videos of His handiwork. *Creation's Voice* accessed through the *Meet the*

Maker page on the website gives 30 days' worth of photos for meditation.

o   Watch nature programmes on television and the internet. Learn more about our wonderful world and use it all as a focus for praise.

o   Have a bird table set up outside your window. Research the best foods to attract different birds, and become an expert on your particular visitors.

o   Use an online or hard-copy concordance, and study what the Bible has to say about creation. This is the site I use: http://www.blueletterbible.org/search.cfm

o   Try your hand at indoor gardening and grow herbs, flowers or even vegetables.

o   If you are in need of physical help to do these things, ask your Heavenly Father to supply sympathetic assistance.

RHYTHMS OF GRACE

HEAR AND RESPOND to the voice of God

o   Get really quiet inside before the Lord.

WHERE DO WE COME FROM?

- o   Centre your attention on Him and ask Him to speak to you.

GOING DEEPER: PERSONAL OR GROUP STUDY

1. This week, look out for things which suggest there is purposeful design undergirding the natural world.

2. Read through the listed Scriptures. Were you struck by anything in particular?

3. Read Romans 1:17-32. What has God revealed about Himself through His creation?

4. What does Hebrew 11:3 teach us about creation? Why is a belief in God as Creator important? What difference does it make to your personal security?

5. Take time to come before the Creator. Turn your heart of affection towards Him, with thanksgiving and praise, and ask Him to speak His beauty and order into any chaotic areas of your life.

6. Try out at least one of the suggestions in the 'Meet the Maker' section.

7. Read Lee Strobel's *The Case for a Creator*,[2] details on the 'Meet the Maker' page of the website. Lee was a convinced sceptic and evolutionist, until he decided to use his skills as an investigative journalist to look at the case for a Creator.

WHERE DO WE COME FROM?

This is a highly readable account of his journey.

END NOTES

[1] Please note, *Meet the Maker* which is a separate page on the website is included in this chapter.

[2] Lee Strobel, (2014) *The Case for a Creator*, Zondervan; Reprint edition

CHAPTER 18

FUEL FOR THE JOURNEY 3

BREAK BREAD

'Breaking bread' (also known as 'Communion' or 'the Lord's Supper') will be explored more fully in the next Rhythms of Grace book. However, it was a specific command of the Lord Jesus, and is an important tool for the journey, so it is included briefly here.

Read Matthew 26:17-30; Luke 22:7-20 and 1 Corinthians 11:23-26.

As we have seen, water baptism makes a single, powerful declaration of our trust in the Jesus' death and resurrection. Breaking bread regularly—even daily—is a powerful way of continuing to proclaim the efficacy of the Lord's death over ourselves and our households.

Re-read *The Power of the Cross* chapter. Bring to the Cross anything which is troubling your conscience and ask for forgiveness [1 John 1:9]. Reflect on how your particular need or circumstance has been met in the Cross.

Using ordinary bread and wine (or grape juice), lift each

up in turn, saying something like:

'Thank You, Lord, for Your death and resurrection. (Break the bread.) Thank You for Your body, which was broken for me.

Eat the bread, sharing it with any other believer present. Then do the same with the wine:

(Lift up the cup of wine.) Thank You for Your blood which was poured out for me, and the Covenant of Blessing You have made with me.

I proclaim the power of Jesus' death over _____, and I receive Your grace, forgiveness, and provision for my needs.

Help me to live in the good of what You have purchased for me. Amen.'

There is no suggestion in the New Testament that a special 'minister' has to be present to validate this.

READ THE WORD 3 (MEDITATION)

If you enjoy reading, you will know that a story (whether true or fictional) is a great vehicle for expressing profound truth, for images can feed our hearts when words are inadequate. So, it is not surprising that God chose story as the primary vehicle in the Bible for conveying the most important truths of all.

A powerful way of meditating on the narrative was taught by Ignatius, an early Christian leader:

Relax and settle into God's presence. Ask Him to touch you.

- o Read the chosen story very slowly, several times, pausing between each reading to take in details, until the narrative saturates your imagination.

- o Using all your senses, allow yourself 'to take part' in the scenes. What can you hear, see, and smell? How does it make you feel? Try to 'participate', without stepping back to analyse.

- o Begin to respond to Jesus: tell Him what you are thinking, and listen to what He's saying.

- o Make notes on the thoughts and impressions which come into your mind.

WORSHIP

Many people connect 'worship' solely with religious services. While these are times, for many religions, when worship is offered in a corporate setting, true Christian worship is a much bigger concept, and something which needs to be developed in the life of a believer on an individual and daily basis.

Both the Hebrew and Greek words used for 'worship' in the Bible have the similar core meaning of 'to prostrate oneself before anyone out of honour', either physically or metaphorically. As we have been abundantly blessed in our restored relationship with our Heavenly Father, our natural response will be one of gratitude, and a desire to honour the One who paid such a price to make it possible.

There isn't a one-size-fits-all expression of devotion. Your worship will be unique to you, your personality, gifts and abilities, and most importantly, something which is done in partnership with the Holy Spirit [John 4:23-24]. Ask Him to lead you.

The following suggestions may give a place to start...

- o Punctuate the day with thanksgiving for God's gifts to you. You can read more about this in Chapter 21.

- o The Book of Psalms is full of expressions of devotion; read until you find something which resonates, then speak it aloud to the Lord, adding your own expressions of love and adoration.

- o There is a wealth of worship music available on YouTube. As you listen, begin to join in, making the songs your own. (It's important that you pay attention to the content of the lyrics. If you feel uncomfortable about any ideas being expressed, discard the song, and find another one.)

- If you like to express yourself creatively, ask the Spirit to help you to worship through different media: perhaps writing love-letters or poetry, playing an instrument or expressive movement; painting or woodwork—the possibilities are endless!

- In addition, you can offer up the actions of the day as love-gifts to the Lord.

And whatever you do, whether in word or deed, do it all in the name of the Lord Jesus, giving thanks to God the Father through Him [Colossians 3: 17].

Therefore, I urge you, brothers and sisters, in view of God's mercy, to offer your bodies as a living sacrifice, holy and pleasing to God – this is your true and proper worship [Romans 12:2].

SECTION 2

CHAPTER 19

CREATING NEW MINDSETS

In the *Introduction*, we saw that Jesus Christ was a perfect example of a man at rest, and that He has opened up the way for us to enter into the same rest that He enjoyed. In the *Foundations* Section, we discovered that through Jesus we can have a personal encounter with God and be filled with His ability; we learned that we find our true identity in relation to Him; and that we can rest in His wonderful provision. This section explores the necessity of putting on new mindsets in order to make progress in our pursuit of rest.

WE'RE ON A JOURNEY

The stories in the Old Testament give graphic pictures of spiritual realities. When the Israelites were delivered from slavery in Egypt, (you can read the account in Exodus 1-14), the imagery portrays the spiritual truth of our passage from death to life. But just as the land on the other side of the Red Sea wasn't Israel's final destination—there was a promised land waiting for them (a land of rest)—neither is it intended that we set up camp just yet! We too are on a

CREATING NEW MINDSETS

journey…

KINGDOM MINDED

Israel's 'promised land' was originally meant to be a theocracy, a place where God would rule over His people; where they would live according to His principles and precepts, and enjoy lives of joy, fruitfulness and prosperity. And the stories also vividly show how sin stopped the nation coming into the fullness of that blessing—and underlined the need for a Saviour, to deliver man from sin, and the world from the powers of darkness.

Jesus was totally 'kingdom-minded', teaching at length about the Kingdom of Heaven, the realm where God rules and where His ways and principles are worked out. In Heaven there is no sin, no sickness, no oppression, no suffering; no darkness at all; it's the sphere where the ways of God preside. When Jesus came to earth, He brought His Kingdom with Him. 'Repent!' He cried, 'For the Kingdom of God is at hand!'

CHANGE YOUR WAY OF THINKING

> *Very truly I tell you, the Son can do nothing by Himself; He can do only what He sees His Father doing, because whatever the Father does the Son also does [John 5:19].*

> *I do nothing on My own but speak just what the Father has taught Me [John 8:28].*

RHYTHMS OF GRACE: A JOURNEY INTO REST

These words you hear are not My own; they belong to the Father who sent Me [John 14:24].

The secret of Jesus' life of rest was that His life was in perfect alignment with His heavenly Father.

We all long to see the wonderful stuff of the Kingdom invade our circumstances; to see God's peace settle on our families or workplaces; to see His healing touch bring restoration to physical, mental and emotional health; and see relationships repaired, long-standing issues resolved, and insecurities dealt with. We want the rest we know these transformations will bring.

In order for the Kingdom of God to come to our personal situations, Jesus was very clear that we have to be 'born again'; otherwise, it's impossible [see John 3: 1-21]. We must have a spiritual rebirth to be able to see spiritual truth. But having had that experience, we also need to change our worldview.

All of us have patterns of thinking, formed over a lifetime, which give the lens through which we view the world and our circumstances. If we are going to walk with God, we have to change that lens to mirror the one He uses; we need to align our way of thinking with the way He thinks; we also have to become kingdom-minded.

The core meaning of the Greek word for 'repentance' is to change the way you think (coupled with contrition and submission to the Lord). In effect, Jesus was saying, 'You need to turn from your old ways, and change your way of thinking so that the Kingdom, the realm of God, can invade your life!'

Faulty thinking always has consequences, whether it's

from ignorance or incorrect beliefs. If I don't know that an electric switch will produce light, I'll live my life in the dark; if I have wrong beliefs about myself and my situation, I will never fulfil my God-given potential; If I have wrong ideas about God and His nature, then I will never receive all that He has for me.

Faulty thinking weighs me down, renders me immobile, and steals my faith—and destiny.

When Jesus was asked what God wants us to do, He didn't reel off a list of worthy activities, but said, rather startlingly, that the real work was to *believe in Him* [John 6:28-29]. And this is 'work', because faith is not an emotion, but a choice which needs developing through application and persistence. It starts with our thought processes, and it takes effort to re-programme our habitual thinking patterns to be places where healthy beliefs can thrive.

So, to see the Kingdom come, I need to develop new mindsets…

KINGDOM MINDSETS

A mindset is a habitual way of thinking, a specific way we look at the world. A diseased mindset fastens me into unhealthy patterns of reaction or behaviour and stops me fulfilling my unique purpose and destiny.

Perhaps some of these diseased thought-patterns trouble you?

- Constant fearful or worried thoughts
- Mental replay of painful situations

- The memory of things said about you in the past
- Negative thoughts about yourself, your abilities, or how others see you

All these unhealthy thinking patterns (and there are many more like them) have the effect of producing stress and stealing our rest. There is also increasing evidence in the medical world that diseased thinking can be responsible for some physical illnesses.

In addition, our behaviour is strongly linked to what we think.

> *For as he thinks in his heart, so is he [Proverbs 23:7 NKJV].*

And Jesus taught:

> *For out of the heart come evil thoughts—murder, adultery, sexual immorality, theft, false testimony, slander [Matthew 15: 19].*

In the world of psychiatry, CBT (Cognitive Behavioural Therapy) has become a popular treatment for people with mental or emotional health issues in recent years. Over a period, unhelpful thought patterns are identified and retrained, in order to affect the way clients behave.

However, the Bible got there a long time ago...

> *Do not conform to the pattern of this world but be transformed by the renewing of your mind. Then you will be able to test and approve what God's will is – His good,*

pleasing and perfect will [Romans 12:2].

These are strong words. If you want personal transformation and changes in your circumstances, you must change your way of thinking. If you want to act differently, you must think differently. If you want to be free from spiritual strongholds of anxiety, fear, guilt, stress, anger—or anything else—you must renew your mind.

THE POWER OF THE IMAGINATION

One of our God-given mental faculties is the power of imagination. When we speak, or hear someone else's words, we immediately form a picture in our mind's eye of the thing mentioned.

The imagination is an essential tool in creating anything; an artist or designer has to have an image, however vague, in their mind to be able to start the design process. It may be discarded, refined or remodelled, but a creation of any sort must have a mental image attached to it.

As our imaginations are created by God, we also need to bring them into alignment with Him and His word. The good news is we can use our imaginations to work with God in creating new mindsets, rather than in opposition.

HOW DO WE RENEW OUR MINDS?

Take it to God. Ask the Holy Spirit to show you your unhealthy thinking patterns. Then take them to the Cross. Jesus took our mental pain and suffering on Himself when

He was crucified. Remember, He was beaten around the head, and suffered the trauma of a vicious crown of thorns? His blood cleanses all the wounds caused by our diseased thinking.

Watch what you feed on. According to experts, our minds are assaulted by more than 50,000 thoughts each day—and a large percentage of these are negative.

Many come from external stimuli: friends, relatives and work colleagues, news reports, TV programmes, magazines, social media, advertising, and music lyrics, to name just a few. Although we can't live in a sanitised bubble away from negative influences, we can monitor what we are feeding on, taking note of which ideas are being sold as 'truth'; and we can limit our intake.

Think on good things every day. Take time out regularly to recalibrate—especially if you have been keeping company with negative people or are being affected by the current news. Re-position your mind with good wholesome thoughts: watch a film, read a book, spend time with your children or in the garden—whatever works for you.

> *Finally, brothers and sisters, whatever is true, whatever is noble, whatever is right, whatever is pure, whatever is lovely, whatever is admirable – if anything is excellent or praiseworthy—think about such things [Philippians 4:8].*

Take every negative thought captive. This one won't

CREATING NEW MINDSETS

happen overnight! When you recognise unhealthy thoughts, lasso them at once and bring them to the Cross, then—and this is important—replace them with good thoughts. Use your sanctified imagination to visualise the truth being worked out in your life.

> *We demolish arguments and every pretension that sets itself up against the knowledge of God, and we take captive every thought to make it obedient to Christ [2 Corinthians 10: 4,5].*

Feed on God's Word. To replace bad thoughts, we have to have good alternatives—we need to fill our minds and hearts with the Word of God. We can…

- read and study the Bible
- listen to audio versions of it
- listen to Bible-based teachings
- read Christian literature
- spend time with people of faith
- frequent Christian websites (such as Rhythms of Grace!) which are full of the Word
- subscribe to Christian blogs or newsletters

Meditate on the Bible. Meditation in the modern world often refers to the types of meditation practised by eastern religions, which involve emptying the mind and entering a state of extreme awareness and inner calm. However, Christianity has a long tradition of its own, which is not about consciousness and emptying the mind, but about fixing the attention of the heart on the Lord and reflecting deeply on His Word.[1] These reflections cause His living Word to become deeply rooted in the heart—and in the thinking. Fixing an over-active mind on the Lord also has a really beneficial calming effect.

> *You will keep him in perfect peace, whose mind is stayed on You, because he trusts in You [Isaiah 26:3 NKJV].*
>
> *And don't for a minute let this Book of The Revelation be out of mind. Ponder and meditate on it day and night, making sure you practice everything written in it. Then you'll get where you're going; then you'll succeed [Joshua 1:8 MSG].*

There are two more essential elements to renewing our minds: *our words*, and *thanksgiving*. These will be explored in the next two chapters.

RHYTHMS OF GRACE

HEAR AND RESPOND to the voice of God

Get very quiet inside. Invite the Holy Spirit to come close. Ask Him to show you what He wants you to focus on, in order to get your thinking in alignment with His. Then ask Him to give you both the desire and the ability to make the changes.

CREATING NEW MINDSETS

> *...for it is God who works in you to will and to act in order to fulfil His good purpose [Philippians 2:13].*

Prayer for change:

> *Lord, I bring You all my diseased thoughts, particularly the ones relating to _____.*
>
> *I confess I have believed them to be truth, and they have shaped my life and behaviour. Forgive me for these thoughts and cleanse my mind with the precious blood of Jesus. Lord Jesus, thank You for dying for me. Thank You for being wounded, so I can be set free. Holy Spirit, please come and help me in my thinking. Help me to replace old thought patterns, and fill me with Your power, so I can be excellent in my mind. Amen*

GOING DEEPER: PERSONAL OR GROUP STUDY

1. What does it mean to 'renew the mind'? Why does Romans 12:2 suggest it is transformational?

2. A well-known quotation from AW Tozer says, *'What comes into our minds when we think about God is the most important thing about us'.*[2] How does what we think about God affect us in our daily lives?

3. Read and reflect on Tozer's book, *The Knowledge of the Holy*.[2] Has anything particularly struck you?

4. Revisit the Gospels. If Jesus was the exact representation of the Father [Hebrews 1:3], what do we learn about the Father by studying Him?
    - How did He relate to people?
    - When was He displeased?
    - What was His attitude towards the trials and distresses of His fellow humans?

END NOTES

[1] The Reflections pages, accessed from the *Creating New Mindsets* page of the website give some starting points for meditation. These are in bite-sized portions, perfect for

busy lives…

[2]AW Tozer, (2016) *Knowledge of the Holy* Bibliotech Press

CHAPTER 20

THE POWER OF THE SPOKEN WORD

Jesus said,

> *'If you hold to My teaching, you are really My disciples. Then you will know the truth, and the truth will set you free'* [John 8: 31-32].

It is the truth we are searching for, truth which sets us free; truth which brings us into that place of internal rest. And holding to the teaching of Jesus, aligning ourselves with God's Word, is the key.

In the last chapter, we looked at the importance of aligning our thought-patterns with God, which is essential in developing internal tranquillity. But in addition to getting our thinking straight, we have to focus on what comes out of our mouths, because there is power in the spoken word.

> *From the fruit of their mouth, a person's stomach is filled; with the harvest of their lips they are satisfied. The tongue has the power of life and death, and those who love it will eat its fruit* [Proverbs 18: 20-21].

'The tongue has the power of life and death'—those are strong words. What comes out of our mouths is determined by the direction of our gaze; and we will see that our words have power, creative power—to fix us in a negative state or open doors to kingdom possibilities. If we focus solely on what we see and experience in the here and now, this will be reflected in what we say; alternatively, if our attention is fixed on what we know of God's perspective, and His promises, then our words will reveal it.

We have to make a choice: to speak words which bring forth 'Kingdom' life; or words which keep us fixed in our present state?

SPEAK KINGDOM REALITY

But what if my situation is truly awful? Shouldn't I tell it as it is?

People often express a concern about being real, and therefore believe that to be authentic we have to say things as they are.

However, there is more than the observable, temporal world; the Bible makes it clear there is also a spiritual realm, which is just as real; in fact, the greater reality. And as Christians, we believe we have been raised up with Christ, and we are seated in heavenly places with Him [Ephesians 2:6], in other words we have access to the realm of Heaven, as well as living in this temporal world. In fact, our job as His children is to release those greater Kingdom realities in our spheres of influence on the earth.

A simple analogy is that when designers understand and

use the law of aerodynamics in making an aircraft, they in effect release a truth which supersedes the law of gravity. Gravity, the principle which states that anything that goes up must come down, remains true and real; but to fly an aeroplane, another law comes into effect which means that it is possible for something to go up and remain there.

Genesis tells the story of an elderly childless couple who were promised a son by God. The book of Romans describes how Abraham faced the temporal 'facts', but was also convinced of a heavenly reality:

> *Without weakening in his faith, he faced the fact that his body was as good as dead – since he was about a hundred years old – and that Sarah's womb was also dead. Yet he did not waver through unbelief regarding the promise of God, but was strengthened in his faith and gave glory to God, being fully persuaded that God had power to do what He had promised [Romans 4: 19-21].*

We live in a fallen world, which is subject to death and decay; however, as His redeemed people, we are also seated in heavenly places with Christ. Facing the temporal 'facts'—not ignoring them—our task is to bring His reality into time and space.

And our words have a huge part to play in that.

THE POWER OF WORDS IN THE BIBLE

The Bible shows clearly that words have creative power. Right at the beginning, at the creation of the world, we read that God spoke the world into existence:

THE POWER OF THE SPOKEN WORD

> *In the beginning, God created the heavens and the earth. Now the earth was formless and empty, darkness was over the surface of the deep, and the Spirit of God was hovering over the waters. And God said, 'Let there be light,' and there was light' [Genesis 1:2-3].*

The book of Hebrews amplifies this thought by suggesting that things in our 'seen' world start their life in the unseen realm; and it is the spoken word which brings them into time and space.

> *By faith, we understand that the universe was formed at God's command, so that what is seen was not made out of what was visible [Hebrews 11:3].*

Jesus, of course, is the Word of God. He is the living, breathing, active articulation of God; eternally God, eternally present, but was revealed in our physical world in bodily form.

And when Jesus spoke with authority, things happened…

The sick were healed, the dead raised, the oppressed were delivered, and storms were calmed.

Mankind was made in the image of God, and our words also have creative power—either for good or evil. [Check out these verses: Proverbs 12:18,25; 13:2-3; 18:20.]

And like the Law of Gravity, it doesn't matter whether you believe in it or not, this divine law still takes an effect, it has been written by God into the very fabric of things. This is the reason non-believers can have great results from 'positive speaking'; they are unwittingly tapping into a created principle. But the 'children of the Kingdom' are supposed to co-operate with the author of these principles, and use them to better effect.

THE PROBLEM WITH NEGATIVE WORDS

Whoever guards his mouth and tongue keeps his soul from troubles [Proverbs 21:23].

We have all had experience of the power of negative words.

- Perhaps you have struggled with things which were spoken over you at school?
- Maybe work colleagues or relatives pass comments which make you feel inadequate?
- Maybe things spoken long ago still replay in your head?
- Or perhaps you speak negatives over yourself: I'm useless at… I can't… I feel so…

Negative words become cages which confine us and choke the life out. They can set the direction for our lives, stopping us from living the life we were designed to live, making us unable to break out and take risks. And they can feel impossible to shake off. The good news is that there is an answer in Jesus—He came to set us free.

Why not take some time today to do a self-audit? How much of your speech is negative? How much is life-giving?

THE POWER OF THE SPOKEN WORD

PARTNER WITH GOD

We read in Romans that 'faith comes by hearing, and hearing by the word of God' [Romans 10:17]. If we want to be people of faith, we have to pay attention to what we say. If faith comes by hearing the word of God, what do we hear ourselves say? What are we speaking out? Words which cause our faith to rise, or words which causes it to plummet?

Right from our very entry into the Christian life, our declarations have been vital; to be properly 'born again' we have to speak!

> *If you declare with your mouth, 'Jesus is Lord,' and believe in your heart that God raised him from the dead, you will be saved. For it is with your heart that you believe and are justified, and it is with your mouth that you profess your faith and are saved [Romans 10: 9-10].*

And if the worlds were framed by what God said, and Jesus, the Word, showed His authority over the powers of darkness by what He said; what if, as His envoys and co-workers, our declarations also have a kingdom impact?

Jesus clearly taught we must speak *to* our 'mountains', not just about them.

> *'Have faith in God,' Jesus answered. 'Truly I tell you, if anyone says to this mountain, "Go, throw yourself into the sea," and does not doubt in their heart but believes that what they say will happen, it will be done for them' [Mark 11:23].*

Interestingly, the Greek words translated 'will happen' in

that verse also carry the meaning of 'be caused to be' or 'come into existence', further suggesting that we take the heavenly realities and speak them into existence in the material world.

This book, and the *Rhythms of Grace* website are full of the promise of a wonderful inheritance, paid for by Jesus, and laid up for us in the heavenly 'bank vaults'; however, we can live like paupers instead of heirs if we do not lay hold of those riches. God is looking for active partnership rather than passivity in faith. And one of the ways we partner with Him is by declaring His truth over our lives and circumstances (sometimes known as 'faith declarations').[1]

> *We do not want you to become lazy, but to imitate those who through faith and patience inherit what has been promised [Hebrews 6:12].*

SPEAK BLESSING OVER OTHERS

Not only are our words to have a positive effect in our own lives, but we are called to release God's blessing over others. When we speak good things to, or about, others; our words become a means of grace to the people around us.

> *Let no unwholesome word proceed from your mouth, but only such a word as is good for edification according to the need of the moment, so that it will give grace to those who hear [Ephesians 4:29].*

Although in general we need to learn how to talk to our Heavenly Father in our own idiomatic style, like in any close relationship, sometimes a pre-written prayer can be useful, such as the one below, to powerfully bless family members and people in your community:

> *I stand in the mighty name of Jesus, as His representative. I bless you (name) with His favour and encompassing love. I bless the work of your hands, that you will prosper in every respect. I bless your family with unity, peace, love and laughter. May the knowledge and revelation of the Lord be upon every member of your household, and may justice and righteousness flow from you. I bless you with health in your bodies, minds and spirits, and may the power of the Holy Spirit rest upon you. Amen (which means 'it shall be so').*

RHYTHMS OF GRACE

HEAR AND RESPOND to the voice of God

Get very quiet inside. Turn your heart towards the Lord and ask Him to come close. Ask Him to show you how much of your speech is negative.

> *Father God, I confess that when I say _____. I am speaking things which bring death, not life. Please forgive me and help me to discover and speak the truth, for*

I want to be in alignment with You. Fill me with the power of Your Holy Spirit, so I can be excellent in my speech. In Jesus' name, I ask it Amen.

Then bring Him negative words which have been spoken over you:

Father God, These words were spoken over me:

_____.

I bring them to You now, and acknowledge that they are not what You think and say about me, and therefore they are not true.

You say _____.

So I choose to throw them down, and I choose to believe the truth. I make the true declaration over myself:

I am _____.

GIVE FREELY because you are blessed

Make it a daily practice to bless someone with your words—family, friends or strangers.

Does the checkout operator look bored? Can you make them laugh? Have you been served well at the filling station? Take time to give praise. Make a phone call and let the

THE POWER OF THE SPOKEN WORD

compliments flow... Words of blessing can change somebody's life.

GOING DEEPER: PERSONAL OR GROUP STUDY

1. Read Proverbs 12:18,25; 13:2-3; 18:20-21; 21:23. What do you learn about the power of your words from these verses?

2. Ask the Lord to show you an area of your life where you need to start declaring His truth over yourself. What does He have to say about your situation? Research and list relevant Scriptures, then put them in the form of personal declarations.[1]

3. Read *The Grace Outpouring* by Roy Godwin.[2] This is the true story of how the practice of speaking blessing over a neighbourhood transformed lives. Are there some aspects of this you can put into practice this week?

END NOTES

[1] There are many resources on *Rhythms of Grace* website devoted to faith-filled declaration; why not check out some of them?

[2] Roy Godwin, (2012) *The Grace Outpouring* David C. Cook; 2nd edition

CHAPTER 21

CHOOSING GRATITUDE

A key aspect of changing our mindsets and developing 'kingdom thinking' is in choosing gratitude. Gratitude produces thanksgiving, and thanksgiving affirms our delight and faith in the God who richly supplies all our needs.

The Greek word for 'thanks' used in the New Testament, is 'eucharisteo'. At its centre are the words 'charis' which means 'grace and favour', and 'chara', which means 'joy'. At the very heart of our thanksgiving is God's grace towards us, and our joyful response.[1]

We thank Him for all we have received, for the many observable blessings which permeate our days, and for the blessings stacked up for us in the heavenly realms which have not yet taken shape in the physical world. Thanksgiving is our declaration of faith that we will see these promised gifts manifested in time and space.

And a thankful heart is a heart at rest.

MORE REASONS TO GIVE THANKS...

1. Thanksgiving 'prepares the way' for us to experience

the 'salvation of God', in all its wonder.

> *He who sacrifices thank-offerings honours Me, and he prepares the way so that I may show him the salvation of God [Psalm 50:23].*

The Hebrew word 'yesha', translated 'salvation' in this verse, (which is at the root of Jesus' name in Hebrew, 'Yeshua') includes deliverance, rescue, safety, welfare, prosperity and victory in its meaning.

Thanksgiving is our vocal declaration of faith in the Lord Jesus, who gave everything so that we could have abundant life. Thanksgiving puts us 'in the `way of God' and is an essential expression of the life of rest and peace.

When Jesus healed the ten lepers [Luke 17:11-19], only one, a Samaritan, came back to thank Him. Jesus' response was to say that his faith had made him 'well'. (This is the Greek word, 'sozo' which includes 'wholeness, deliverance, restoration and salvation' in its meaning.) Not only did the Samaritan receive healing like his friends, but thanksgiving opened the door to a whole box of goodies!

It's also sobering to note that the opposite of thanksgiving—grumbling and complaining, was enough to keep the Israelites out of the Promised Land [Numbers 11; 13-14:4]!

2. Giving thanks is also the way we acknowledge the presence of God:

> *Enter His gates with thanksgiving and His courts with praise; give thanks to Him and praise His name [Psalm*

100:4].

He is always with us as we learned in the chapter, 'Experiencing God's Presence', but as we give thanks for that truth, we position ourselves for a greater experience of it.

3. Lastly, and most importantly, thanksgiving pleases Him:

I will praise God's name in song and glorify Him with thanksgiving. This will please the Lord more than an ox, more than a bull with its horns and hoofs [Psalm 69:30,31].

FOUR AREAS TO FOCUS OUR THANKS

DAILY LOVE GIFTS

God loves us passionately, and our lives are filled with demonstrations of His love: that sunset, this flower; that child's embrace, this piece of music...

ALL SPIRITUAL BLESSINGS

We have also received every spiritual blessing in the heavenly realms [Ephesians 1:3], where we are seated with Christ! We are to partner with Him in releasing these blessings in our spheres of influence.

Therefore, I tell you, whatever you ask for in prayer, believe that you have received it, and it will be yours [Mark 11:24].

When we receive a gift, we thank the giver. As we give thanks for our blessings in Christ, we are not only showing gratitude, we are giving voice to our faith that we have received from God, (see previous chapter) and that we will see those gifts being realised in our physical world.

DAILY FRUSTRATIONS

Our lives are also filled with petty irritations and frustrations: the car that breaks down, the spilled soup, the crying toddler, the slow driver...

However, Scripture is unequivocal,

Rejoice always, pray continually, give thanks in all circumstances; for this is God's will for you in Christ Jesus [1 Thessalonians 5:16-18].

And the reason is this:

We know that all things work together for good to those who love God, to those who are called according to His purpose [Romans 8:28 NKJV].

God works all things together. All things. This being so, we can be thankful for everything, even the annoying parts of our day, believing He is working out His purpose in our lives, and covers everything with His grace.

Allowing thanksgiving to flow in the ordinary mini-trials of life enables us to experience rest and peace in His arms, and to release that grace to others—the driver who cuts us up, the telesales person... and our nearest and dearest!

TRIALS AND DEVASTATION

Then what about the big stuff? We live in a fallen world and devastation is all around. But the New Testament is clear: Jesus came to destroy the Devil's works [John 10:10; 1 John 3:8] and gave His followers the same mandate [Mark 16:15-18]. Victory was won decisively on the Cross, and believers have been tasked with enforcing it.

However, it is a steep learning-curve, and we have to grow in the faith and authority to win our battles. At those times when the Evil One appears to triumph, thanksgiving marks our trust in the One who covers everything with His grace and love, and is able to transform the most diabolical situation, even death on a cross!

> *And we know that in all things God works for the good of those who love Him, who have been called according to His purpose [Romans 8:28].*

In those challenging times, we don't have to understand everything or be able to see how things will work out; we can find rest and peace in the arms of the One who knows it all—for He will never leave us or forsake us [Hebrews 13:5].

RHYTHMS OF GRACE

HEAR AND RESPOND to the voice of God

Get very quiet inside.

- Turn your heart towards the Lord and ask Him to come close. Ask Him to…
- show you the blessings which surround you
- give you revelation of the wonderful things Jesus purchased for you
- remind you to be thankful when life is annoying
- give you deep peace when crises hit
- Then listen…

GET IN THE FLOW of His Spirit

Thanksgiving is to flow from inside-out. Ask the Holy Spirit to well up in you and overflow in a river of gratitude.

GOING DEEPER: PERSONAL OR GROUP STUDY

1. How is thanksgiving related to faith? How does it affect your rest? Why do you think gratitude is a choice rather than a feeling?

2. Read Numbers 11; 13-14:4. Why do you think grumbling and complaining kept the Israelites out of the Promised Land?

3. Recap on the blessings outlined in previous chapters and spend some time giving thanks for the wonderful inheritance Jesus has purchased for you.

4. What do you think the difference is between thanksgiving and praise? Why do you think it is important that we verbalise our gratitude?

5. As well as verbalising thanks, consider responding to your blessings creatively—a book of thanksgiving, a psalm, a song, a painting, a photograph, or a dance for example, (the possibilities are endless). The act of recording makes us slow down, and reinforces the sense of blessing in us, but also becomes another expression of worship.

END NOTES

[1] Ann Voskamp, (2021) *One Thousand Gifts*, Thomas Nelson Publishers; 10th Anniversary edition

CHAPTER 22

NOTES ON DISCERNMENT

The internet age has brought many benefits, among them, access to a rich variety of Christian ministry. However, the flip side of this abundance is a cacophony of voices, all demanding attention. The resulting confusion can be debilitating. How do we sift through all the voices, all claiming revelation, in order to take hold of what is good, and avoid being led astray?

Here are some simple principles. The 'speaker' cited below, may be a Christian leader, a prophet, a ministry, a musician, a writer, or simply a friend or acquaintance.

1. Long ago, the Church Fathers gave us the non-negotiable bones of our faith:

We believe in one God,
the Father Almighty,
Maker of Heaven and earth,
of all things visible and invisible.

And in one Lord Jesus Christ,
the only Son of God,
begotten from the Father before all ages,

God from God,
Light from Light,
true God from true God,
begotten, not made;
of the same essence as the Father.
Through Him all things were made.

For us and for our salvation
He came down from Heaven;
He became incarnate by the Holy Spirit and the virgin Mary,
and was made human.
He was crucified for us under Pontius Pilate;
He suffered and was buried.
The third day He rose again, according to the Scriptures.
He ascended to Heaven
and is seated at the right hand of the Father.
He will come again with glory
to judge the living and the dead.
His kingdom will never end.

And we believe in the Holy Spirit,
the Lord, the giver of life.
He proceeds from the Father and the Son,
and with the Father and the Son is worshipped and glorified.
He spoke through the prophets.
We believe in one holy catholic (universal) and apostolic church.
We affirm one baptism for the forgiveness of sins.
We look forward to the resurrection of the dead,
and to life in the world to come. Amen.

Nicene Creed (325 AD)

NOTES ON DISCERNMENT

But added to those foundational truths are myriad interpretations of Scripture, all with different emphases according to revelation. And because *no* one ministry or stream has all the revelation—Paul says we know and see in part [1 Corinthians 13:9]—it is important that none of us should blindly follow anyone. We have been given the Holy Spirit for the very purpose of guiding us into all truth. Never ignore His gentle pressure; if something feels 'off', don't ignore it, check it out in Scripture. The internet is an invaluable resource for these purposes.

2. Look first at the attitude of the 'speaker': are they humble? Are they full of grace and love? Do they reflect the character of Christ? Remember, the only people Jesus had harsh words for, were the religious, the self-satisfied and the judgemental.

> *Therefore, as God's chosen people, holy and dearly loved, clothe yourselves with compassion, kindness, humility, gentleness and patience [Colossians 3:12].*

Then think about what is being said. James has an important perspective here.

> *With the tongue we praise our Lord and Father, and with it we curse human beings, who have been made in God's likeness. Out of the same mouth come praise and cursing. My brothers and sisters, this should not be. Can both fresh water and salt water flow from the same spring? My brothers and sisters, can a fig-tree bear olives, or a grapevine bear figs? Neither can a salt spring produce fresh water [James 3:9-12].*

But the wisdom that comes from heaven is first of all pure; then peace-loving, considerate, submissive, full of mercy and good fruit, impartial and sincere. Peacemakers who sow in peace reap a harvest of righteousness. [James 3:17-18]

3. Does the teaching or opinion agree with the 'main and plain' in Scripture, particularly with what Jesus said and did in the Gospels. He was the exact representation of the Father, so it's a good place to start.

4. What fruit is in evidence? Does the 'speaker' produce the character of humility, grace and love in the lives of others; or people who are unteachable, strident, judgemental or legalistic?

Make a tree good and its fruit will be good, or make a tree bad and its fruit will be bad, for a tree is recognised by its fruit… For the mouth speaks what the heart is full of. A good man brings good things out of the good stored up in him… [Matthew 12:33-37]

5. Finally, don't just drink from one 'well'. As no ministry, stream or person has complete revelation, or a perfect grasp on truth, it is important to hear from other Christian worldviews—with the above safety factors in place. There is a rich treasure to be found in the family of God; let's search it out!

NOTES ON DISCERNMENT

Learning to discern where people are coming from, helps us guard against getting caught up in error, and the resultant hurt. We need to remove ourselves from anything toxic, without flaring up in self-righteous judgement; and then take and bless what is good, and, realising that we are all imperfect learners—pray for each other.

CONCLUSION

All over the world, people are searching for peace in very uncertain times. It is my conviction, that despite being awash with advice ranging from the trite and foolish, to thoughtful and beneficial, true rest can ultimately only be found through accepting God's invitation to journey with Him, specifically through receiving the provision He has made for us in Jesus Christ.

I hope as you come to the end of this course, you feel established on this journey of a lifetime, and in your relationship with your Heavenly Father who loves you so dearly. I also hope you will never 'settle' but will keep pushing forward to receive everything the Lord Jesus paid such a price to purchase for you.

God bless you,

Kate Waterman

CONCLUSION

SHARE YOUR THOUGHTS

Do get in touch with me and share your thoughts on *Rhythms of Grace: a Journey into Rest* by emailing: journeyintorest@gmail.com

Please submit your review of this book at Amazon: https://www.amazon.co.uk/, https://www.amazon.com/ or your country-specific site. And if you have been blessed or inspired by this book, please recommend to your friends, and on social media.

THE WEBSITE

If you haven't visited the website of the same name yet, please do. You will find an abundance of resources, as well as a weekly blog to help you in your journey. It can be found at https://www.rhythmsofgraceuk.org

RHYTHMS OF GRACE: A JOURNEY INTO REST PART 2

The last section of the website, *Kingdom Living,* will be published in book format in due course. If you would like to be notified when it becomes available: email the above address, marking the Subject as *notify*.

ABOUT THE AUTHOR

Kate Waterman lives with her husband in the beautiful border-country between Scotland and England, where she divides her time between writing, painting and enjoying country living. She has been a Jesus-follower for over 40 years, and along with her husband, has many years' experience in various aspects of Christian ministry. In addition to being a mother, and grandmother, Kate has also worked as a primary school teacher and in care for the elderly. She can be contacted through her website: https://www.rhythmsofgraceuk.org or by email at journeyintorest@gmail.com

Printed in Great Britain
by Amazon